MAMMOTHS

MAMMOTHS

ICE-AGE GIANTS

Dr. Larry D. Agenbroad and Lisa Nelson

Lerner Publications Company • Minneapolis

To all those who appreciate the proboscideans, especially mammoths

We owe a debt of gratitude to three especially knowledgeable researchers who share a fascination with mammoths. Their review of our manuscript prevented some embarrassing errors and helped clarify what we know about mammoths. A special thank-you to Gary Haynes, Professor, College of Arts and Science at the University of Nevada-Reno; Adrian Lister, Lecturer in Biology, University College, London; and Paul Martin, Professor, Department of Geosciences, University of Arizona.

Copyright © 2002 by Lerner Publications Company

This book is available in two editions:
Library binding by Lerner Publications Company,
  a division of Lerner Publishing Group
Soft cover by First Avenue Editions,
  an imprint of Lerner Publishing Group
241 First Avenue North
Minneapolis, Minnesota 55401 U.S.A.

Website address: www.lernerbooks.com

Library of Congress Cataloging-in-Publication Data

Agenbroad, Larry D.
    Mammoths: ice-age giants / written by Larry D. Agenbroad and Lisa Nelson.
       p.   cm. (Discovery!)
    Includes bibliographical references and index.
    ISBN: 0–8225–2862–2 (lib. bdg. : alk. paper)
    ISBN: 0–8225–0470–7 (pbk. : alk. paper)
    1. Woolly mammoth—Juvenile literature. (1. Mammoths. 2. Paleontology.)
    I. Nelson, Lisa W. II. Title. III. Discovery! (Lerner Publications Company)
    QE822.P8 A38 2002
    569'.67—dc21   2001001147

Manufactured in the United States of America
1 2 3 4 5 6 – JR – 07 06 05 04 03 02

CONTENTS

WHY STUDY MAMMOTHS?

Mammoths reigned as giants on land for more than three million years. Many were as tall as a house and weighed as much as a semi truck. Their huge ivory tusks dipped and curved to a length of 10 feet (3 meters). Adult mammoths feared no predators—except perhaps humans.

Most mammoths lived during the Pleistocene epoch—a span of time when long periods of intense cold were occasionally interrupted by shorter cycles of warmer weather. The Pleistocene epoch ended about eleven thousand years ago. By that time, the mammoths had nearly vanished. Extinction claimed these Ice-Age giants.

Mammoths and dinosaurs shared a similar fate. They were among the largest animals on land, and extinction wiped out both of them. But that's pretty much where the similarity ends. Dinosaurs became extinct millions of years before mammoths arrived on the scene. Unlike the reptilian dinosaurs, mammoths were mammals and, for a while, they coexisted with humans. Like mice, muskrats, horses, hares, and other modern mammals, mammoths gave birth to their young and nursed their babies with mother's milk.

Scientists know more about the physical appearance and lifestyle of mammoths than they do about dinosaurs because

Ancient relatives of modern-day African and Asian elephants, mammoths (facing page) *lived alongside the earliest humans thousands of years ago.*

abundant, well-preserved mammoth remains have been discovered. These include frozen carcasses—complete with skin, hair, and internal organs, including the heart. Researchers have also uncovered intact mammoth skeletons buried on land and bones submerged in the sea. They have even pieced together what the giant animals ate by studying mammoth dung found in caves. So far, mammoth remains have been found only on the continents of Africa, Europe, Asia, and North America. No signs of mammoths have been discovered in the Southern Hemisphere.

Mammoths fascinate people of all ages. A mother and daughter look at a mammoth skeleton found in 1999 in Florida's Aucilla River.

By studying mammoth remains, paleontologists (scientists who study evidence of past life on Earth) have learned that many different kinds of mammoths roamed the Northern Hemisphere. There were the woolly mammoths whose hairy overcoats offered warm protection from the arctic cold. There were the larger, less hairy Columbian mammoths that favored the warmer climate of North America. There were even island-dwelling miniature mammoths.

Scientists have learned a great deal by studying mammoth remains, but that is not their only source of knowledge. Ancient peoples who lived alongside mammoths also left behind clues. Cave paintings—some in surprising detail—captured the first human observations of mammoths. In addition, ancient artifacts reveal that humans used mammoth bones and tusks as tools and for ornamentation. They even built entire huts out of mammoth bones.

There is plenty of evidence that humans hunted the great mammoths. However, the question remains: How did mammoths become extinct? Did humans hunt the Ice-Age giants to extinction? Perhaps the mammoths were killed by Earth's changing climate or by disease, or perhaps something else—something scientists don't yet know about—was responsible. Scientists would also like to know why elephants, close relatives of the mammoths, continue to survive, while mammoths died out.

So far, researchers have not been able to solve any of these mysteries. That is why they continue to probe for clues. In the end, what scientists learn about mammoths and their extinction may help all of us to better understand our place in the world. Scientific discoveries may also help us find ways to save many of the creatures that are now in danger of extinction.

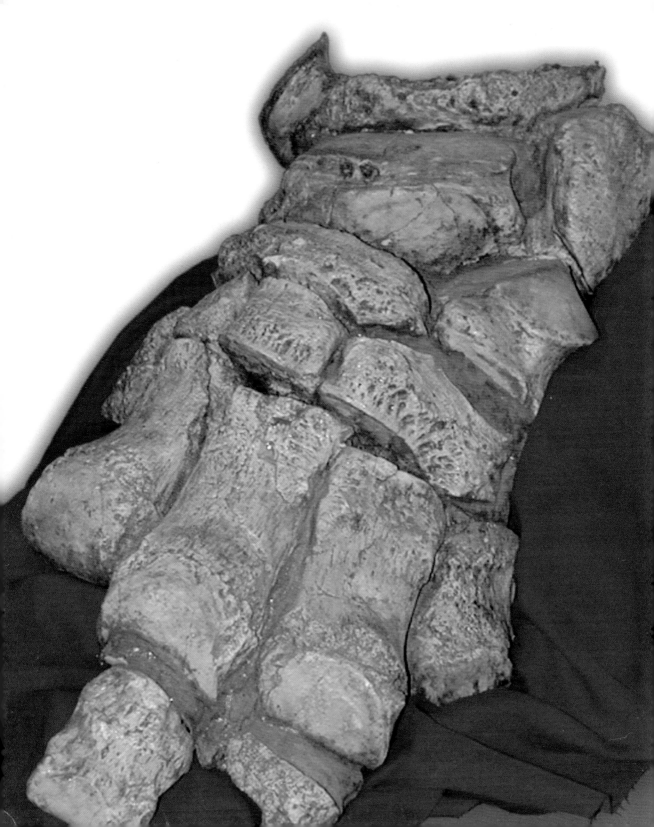

Chapter One

A CLOSER LOOK AT MAMMOTHS

Mammoths and modern elephants are closely related, but mammoths were not the ancestors of elephants. The origins of mammoths and elephants trace back to Africa. Mammoths and elephants both belong to a group of mammals called the proboscideans. The name comes from the word *proboscis,* which means "long, flexible snout"—as in the trunk of the mammoth and the elephant.

Mammoths and modern elephants also belong to a subgroup of proboscideans called the elephantids. The Asian and African elephants are the only two surviving species of elephantids.

The mammoth, the African elephant, and the Asian elephant each evolved separately between three million and five million years ago. So while we can call mammoths and elephants close "cousins," we cannot say that elephants descended from mammoths.

Oddly enough, the closest living relatives of elephants are the aquatic sea cow and the rock-dwelling hyrax, which looks like an overgrown guinea pig. An elephant, a sea cow, and a hyrax seem as different from each other as night and day. So how can they be related? While they don't look too similar on the outside, these animals share some common internal features.

By closely examining bones, such as those in this Columbian mammoth foot (facing page), *scientists can determine the mammoth's modern-day relatives, including the hyrax.*

One similarity is in the carpal, or wrist, bones. The wrist bones of the elephant, sea cow, and hyrax are stacked one atop the other, while the wrist bones of most other mammals are arranged in a staggered fashion. The hearts of these three animals are also similar, and they differ from those of other mammals. An elephant's heart looks like a valentine heart, with two humps instead of the one hump found in most mammals' hearts. Also, the ear and leg bones of the hyrax are similar to those of the elephant. By studying the genes and proteins of the elephant and the hyrax, scientists have confirmed that the two mammals share a common ancestry. The ancestor of the elephant, sea cow, and hyrax was probably no bigger than a small dog and may have first appeared about sixty-five million years ago.

PROBOSCIDEAN EVOLUTION

The earliest proboscidean was a swamp-dwelling creature that lived fifty million years ago. Known as *Moeritherium*, its remains were discovered at Lake Moeris in Egypt. *Moeritherium* was about the size of a pig and looked similar to a hippopotamus. Although it had no trunk, *Moeritherium* had small, hippolike tusks.

From these beginnings, proboscideans began to migrate in all directions, populating what are now Africa, Eurasia, and the Americas. These animal populations began adapting to the specific environmental and climatic conditions of their habitats. As a result, a multitude of species evolved. Most of the 165 or so species of proboscideans can be organized into four main groups: deinotheres, mammutids, gomphotheres, and elephantids—the group that includes mammoths and modern elephants (see diagram on page 14). The deinotheres appeared about forty-five million years ago. The earliest mammutids

The stocky, piglike Moeritherium *had a small protrusion that later evolved into a trunk. This proboscidean is the predecessor to mammoths.*

evolved about twenty-five million years ago, followed by the gomphotheres about fifteen million years ago, and finally, the elephantids about eight million years ago.

Deinotherium, the most well-known deinothere, was about the size of a present-day elephant and had a trunk and downward-curving tusks that grew out of its lower jaw. Why did this proboscidean have "upside-down" tusks? Scientists don't know for sure, but some researchers have suggested that the animal may have used them to dig up underwater vegetation.

Although the mammutids, or mastodons, and mammoths lived at the same time, they were not very closely related. The mastodon was shorter and stockier than the mammoth, and its head was more sloped than the high-crowned skull of the mammoth.

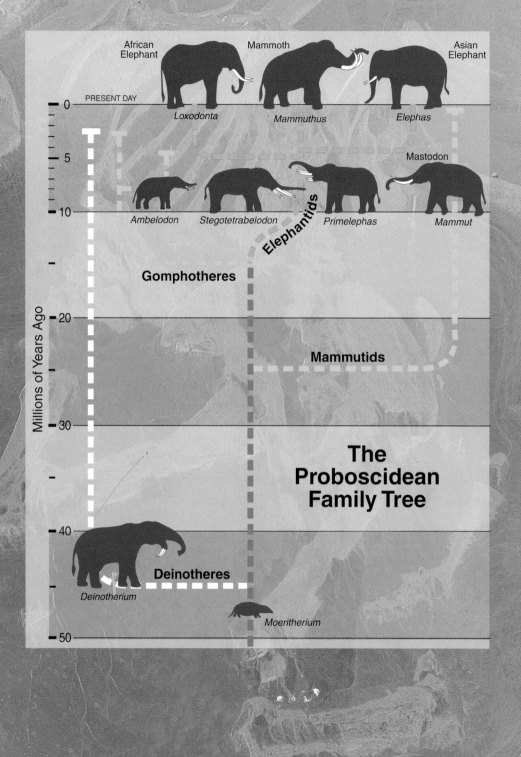

African Elephant
Loxodonta

Mammoth
Mammuthus

Asian Elephant
Elephas

PRESENT DAY

Ambelodon

Stegotetrabelodon

Primelephas

Mastodon
Mammut

Elephantids

Gomphotheres

Mammutids

Millions of Years Ago

The Proboscidean Family Tree

Deinotheres

Deinotherium

Moeritherium

0
5
10
20
30
40
50

Below: *An illustration of a mammoth (on left) and a mastodon (on right) shows some of their physical differences.*

Above: *Compare the flat, ridged mammoth molar on the left to the pointed mastodon molar on the right.*

The easiest way to distinguish between the two creatures is by looking at their teeth. The mammoth's large, flat teeth were reinforced with enamel plates—a perfect design for shearing and grinding coarse grasses. The mastodon's teeth had high pointed ridges, allowing it to eat a wider variety of plant materials, including branches, twigs, leaves, roots, and melons.

The gomphotheres were a large and varied group of proboscideans. They ranged in size from 3 to 10 feet (1 to 3 meters) tall, and many species had a long head and neck as well as highly specialized jaws. One of the later members of this group, *Ambelodon*, is also known as the "shovel tusker." At the end of its long, shovel-shaped jaw, *Ambelodon* had flat lower incisors that looked like giant buck teeth. The animal probably ate by grasping

Four species of gomphothere are illustrated here. They are (from left to right) Trilophodon, Ambelodon, Ocalientinus, *and* Torynobelodon.

aquatic vegetation with its trunk, severing the roots with its protruding teeth, and then scooping the food into its mouth.

The earliest elephantids were the four-tusked *Stegotetrabelodon* and *Primelephas. Stegotetrabelodon* dates back eight million years, while *Primelephas* lived between six million and three million years ago. Both animals had the characteristic flat-ridged molars of the mammoth and the modern elephant.

Between five and three million years ago, the elephantids split into three main groups: *Loxodonta, Elephas,* and *Mammuthus. Loxodonta* produced the modern African elephant, *Loxodonta africana*. It has been proposed that there is a second African species, *Loxodonta cyclotis,* which is genetically different from *Loxodonta africana.* From *Elephas* emerged the Asian elephant, *Elephas maximus.* Meanwhile, *Mammuthus* gave rise to the mammoths.

Telling Geologic Time

Earth is about 4.6 billion years old. Fossil evidence suggests that very simple life-forms appeared on the planet about 3.9 billion years ago, but the first animals did not evolve until about 600 million years ago. Scientists who study the evolution of life on Earth have divided the last 575 million years into smaller units called eras, periods, and epochs. During each of these time units, conditions on Earth were unique, and so were the creatures that inhabited our world. Mammoths lived in the Pleistocene epoch of the Quaternary period during the Cenozoic era.

GEOLOGIC TIMESCALE

ERA	PERIOD	EPOCH	MILLIONS OF YEARS AGO
Cenozoic (Age of Mammals)	Quaternary	Holocene	0.01 to present
		Pleistocene	1.8 to 0.01
	Tertiary	Pliocene	5.3 to 1.8
		Miocene	23.8 to 5.3
		Oligocene	33.7 to 23.8
		Eocene	54.8 to 33.7
		Paleocene	65 to 54.8
Mesozoic* (Age of Reptiles)	Cretaceous		144 to 65
	Jurassic		206 to 144
	Triassic		248 to 206
Paleozoic* (Early Animals)	Permian		290 to 248
	Carboniferous		354 to 290
	Devonian		417 to 354
	Silurian		443 to 417
	Ordovician		490 to 443
	Cambrian		540 to 490

* Each period of the Mesozoic and Paleozoic eras can also be divided into epochs, but they have not been listed in this table because proboscideans lived only during the Cenozoic era.

Many people think elephants evolved from mammoths, but careful research has shown otherwise. Early elephants developed separately from mammoths, and the two groups were alive at the same time. Nevertheless, mammoths and elephants do share many common features. In fact, in some ways, Asian elephants are more similar to mammoths than they are to African elephants.

THE MAMMOTH FAMILY TREE

The group of elephantids known as *Mammuthus* began migrating from Africa into western Europe about three million years ago. Scientists call the first mammoth species to arrive in Europe and later in North America *Mammuthus meridionalis*. This animal is also known as the ancestral mammoth. Scientists believe it was the ancestor of all the species of mammoths that lived on the European, Asian, and North American continents. Based on skeletal remains, *Mammuthus meridionalis* was about 13 feet (4 meters) tall—bigger than most modern elephants. Plant remains found with the bones suggest that Earth's climate was mild when this mammoth lived.

Mammuthus meridionalis survived for about two million years. It died out as Earth's climate cooled and open grasslands, or steppes, replaced the mammoth's warm tropical forest habitat. The demise of the ancestral mammoth gave rise to its descendants, *Mammuthus trogontherii* (the steppe mammoth) in Eurasia and *Mammuthus imperator* (the Imperial mammoth) in North America. The steppe mammoth and Imperial mammoth were true giants. At about 14 feet (4.3 meters), they stood taller than any other mammoth that ever lived. Eventually, these mammoths faced the same fate as their ancestors—extinction.

In Europe, mammoth evolution culminated with *Mammuthus primigenius,* the famed woolly mammoth. Some woolly mammoths traveled from their homeland in Siberia to Alaska, Canada, and the Great Lakes region of the United States. The last mammoth to live in North America was *Mammuthus columbi,* the Columbian mammoth. By the end of the Pleistocene epoch, about ten thousand years ago, mammoths had nearly vanished. However, for several thousand years, a few isolated populations of mammoths apparently continued to survive. Remains of a small woolly mammoth on Wrangel Island, north of Russian Siberia, indicate that the animal died just 3,700 years ago—about the time the Egyptians were building the pyramids.

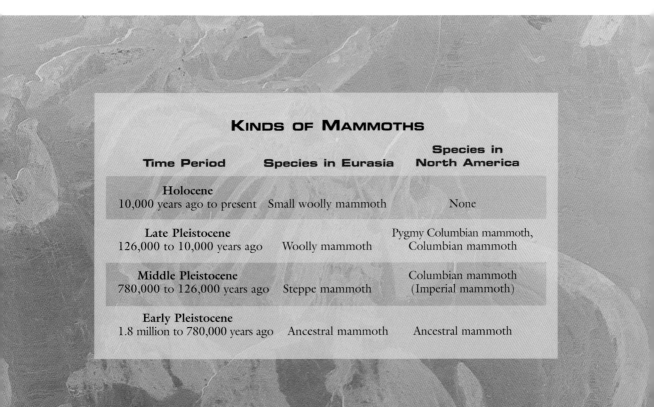

KINDS OF MAMMOTHS

Time Period	Species in Eurasia	Species in North America
Holocene 10,000 years ago to present	Small woolly mammoth	None
Late Pleistocene 126,000 to 10,000 years ago	Woolly mammoth	Pygmy Columbian mammoth, Columbian mammoth
Middle Pleistocene 780,000 to 126,000 years ago	Steppe mammoth	Columbian mammoth (Imperial mammoth)
Early Pleistocene 1.8 million to 780,000 years ago	Ancestral mammoth	Ancestral mammoth

Chapter Two

MAMMOTH TRAVELS

The first mammoths originated about 3.5 million years ago in Africa and slowly migrated into Europe, Asia, and finally North America. If you take a look at a map of the world, you might wonder how mammoths could have traveled from Siberia on the northeastern edge of Asia, across the Bering Strait, and into Alaska on the northwestern tip of North America. Although they were good swimmers, it's doubtful that mammoths could have paddled 60 miles (97 kilometers) across the Bering Strait. To understand how mammoths ended up in North America, you need to know what the world looked like when mammoths were on the move.

The Pleistocene is often referred to as the Ice Age. During that time, vast sheets of ice called glaciers covered much of northern Europe, Asia, and North America. In reality, a series of ice ages occurred during the Pleistocene. Throughout this epoch, glaciers periodically advanced and then retreated across the continents. At their peak, the glaciers covered more than 30 percent of the land on Earth. The periods between glacial advances—when temperatures warmed and glaciers shrank—are called interglacials. For the most part, interglacials were much shorter than the colder glacial periods.

Pleistocene glaciers formed when snow accumulated faster than it melted, and ice built up underneath the snow. The sheer

Giant sheets of ice covered much of the world during the time mammoths roamed Earth.

weight of the snow pushed out the edge of the glacier so that it flowed like a river of ice. The glacier-forming snow was produced when water that evaporated from the oceans came into contact with the cold atmosphere and fell as snow. During cold glacial periods, sea level dropped as more oceanic water evaporated to produce snow. Glacial advances could have caused sea level to fall by as much as 300 feet (90 meters) in some parts of the world. During the warmer interglacials, the snow melted and sea level rose again.

When sea level fell during cold glacial periods, the Bering Strait separating Siberia and Alaska became dry land that mammoths and other animals could travel across. This land bridge was called central Beringia. Throughout the Pleistocene, central Beringia was exposed periodically as glaciers advanced and retreated and sea level rose and fell.

How did mammoths get from Alaska and Canada to the continental United States? Scientists believe that, during most of the Pleistocene, two vast ice sheets covered most of North America, extending as far south as the Missouri River. During interglacials, as the ice sheets retreated, an ice-free corridor opened between the two ice sheets, giving mammoths in Alaska and Canada easy access to land to the south.

Mammoths filtered into North America and traveled as far south as Costa Rica. The mammoths' distant cousin, the gomphothere, was able to head even farther south and cross another land bridge between Mexico and South America. With its cusped—or pointed—molars, the gomphothere could munch on the twigs and leaves of bushes that grew throughout the southern portion of Central America. The mammoth didn't follow the gomphothere's trail, however, because its flat teeth were better suited to grazing in grasslands.

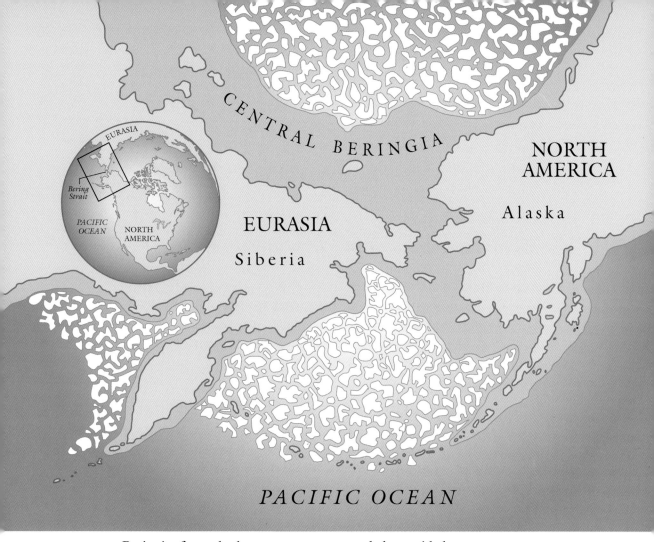

EURASIA

Siberia

CENTRAL BERINGIA

NORTH AMERICA

Alaska

PACIFIC OCEAN

Beringia, formed when ocean waters receded, provided a passageway between Eurasia and North America for migrating mammoths. The globe (inset) shows the modern-day Bering Strait.

Proboscideans weren't the only animals migrating into North America from Eurasia. Bison, elk, and humans were also making the trek—and the traffic wasn't just one way. While mammoths headed east into North America, horses and camels migrated west to Eurasia. That's right, large camels were once native to North America. Although these animals eventually died out, a group of close cousins—camelids, such as vicuñas and guanacos—still survive in South America. (Llamas and alpacas are tame camelids.)

SOMETIMES SMALLER IS BETTER

Although mammoths and other proboscideans probably didn't swim from Eurasia to North America, they may have paddled out to islands just a few miles off the coast. Asian elephants have been known to swim to islands they cannot even see. They are guided by the aroma of ripening fruit and vegetation. Some elephants have been recorded swimming to islands up to 30 miles (48 kilometers) away. Ancient proboscideans were most certainly just as seaworthy as modern elephants.

Scientists have observed Asian elephants swimming in the ocean. Perhaps mammoths swam to islands close to the mainland.

The Key deer of Florida is an example of dwarfing.

In some cases, island-dwelling proboscideans evolved smaller bodies. Evolutionary dwarfing is not uncommon on islands. Food is often scarce, and smaller animals require less food. Smaller size particularly favors animals during times of natural stress, such as droughts or lightning fires, that temporarily destroy vegetation. Because large-animal predators do not live on islands, proboscideans didn't have to grow to intimidating sizes to stay safe. A modern example of dwarfing is the Key deer on islands off the coast of Florida. They are half the size of their white-tailed cousins on the Florida mainland.

Miniature proboscideans evolved independently on various islands worldwide. These include dwarf elephants from islands in the Mediterranean Sea and pygmy mammoths from the Channel Islands off the coast of California. Scientists believe dwarf elephants and pygmy mammoths began as full-size species and shrank to half their original size over several hundred years.

These skeletons of pygmy elephants were discovered on Sicily.

The oldest and smallest dwarf elephant remains have been re-
trieved from caves on Sicily and Malta. The bones date back
five hundred thousand years, to a time when Sicily and Malta
were one island. This particular elephant stood only 3 feet (1
meter) tall, about the size of a Saint Bernard dog.

The most abundant miniature mammoth remains—pygmy
Columbian mammoths—have turned up on three of the California Channel Islands: San Miguel, Santa Rosa, and Santa
Cruz. As Ice-Age glaciers spread over the land, sea level
dropped and increased the surface area of California's Channel

Islands, forming one "super" island known as Santarosae. Mammoths, attracted by the scent of vegetation, swam out to these islands. Eventually, the climate changed, glaciers started melting, sea level rose, and only the highest points of Santarosae protruded above the ocean waters—turning the super island into four smaller, separate islands. Over time, mammoths marooned on these islands adapted to their smaller habitats by developing smaller bodies.

The most complete specimen of a pygmy mammoth was discovered on Santa Rosa in 1994. The skeleton is 95 percent complete—missing only its right tusk, some vertebrae, and portions of its skull and pelvis. The orientation of the skeleton when it was found suggests that the animal lay down on its left

On barren Santa Rosa Island, off the coast of Santa Barbara, California, paleontologists found evidence of pygmy mammoths.

side with its legs stretched out and never got up. Sand covered the carcass and preserved the remains for more than twelve thousand years before erosion exposed the bones once again. Measurements of the mammoth's teeth and bones reveal that it was a fifty-year-old male. Abnormal bone growth shows that the mammoth suffered from arthritis in its right hind foot.

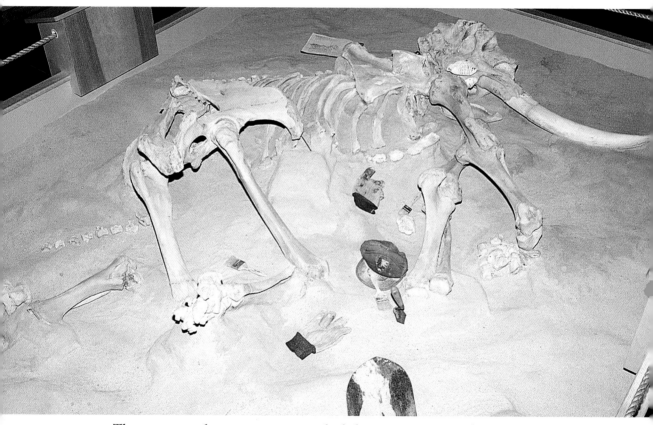

The most complete pygmy mammoth skeleton ever recovered was unearthed on Santa Rosa Island in 1994. The adjacent glove and tools show the relative size of the skeleton.

It's very likely that groups of Columbian mammoths migrated to Santarosae over a period of ten thousand to fifty thousand years. Some remains of full-size Columbian mammoths have been found on the Channel Islands, but the ratio of skeletal evidence is about 10 to 1 in favor of the pygmy mammoths. Three possibilities may explain the presence of the full-size Columbian mammoths on the islands:

1. they were late migrants to the Channel Islands;
2. they were contemporaries of the pygmy mammoths that had just swum out from the California mainland;
3. they represented the intermediate stages in the dwarfing process.

There is no evidence that pygmy mammoths ever swam back to the California mainland.

Chapter Three

WHEN MAMMOTHS RULED

Most of what we know about how mammoths looked, what they ate, and how they lived comes from the abundant remains of the woolly and Columbian mammoths. These remains have shown us that mammoths were vegetarians and spent most of their time foraging for food. Columbian mammoths ate more than 300 pounds (140 kilograms) of plant material each day. While grass was a dietary staple, mammoths also ate other plants, including shrubs and tree branches.

A MAMMOTH'S TEETH

The teeth of a full-grown mammoth were large—about as big as a man's size twelve shoe box. They had to be big so that the mammoth could chew the huge quantities of grass it consumed.

While humans have only two sets of teeth in a lifetime, the mammoth had six. However, the mammoth had only four fully exposed teeth in its mouth at any one time—two in the upper jaw and two in the lower jaw. When one set of teeth started to wear down, a new set of molars erupted from behind and pushed out the teeth in front. This conveyor-belt replacement of teeth continued until the sixth and final set appeared.

Volunteers and paleontologists unearth mammoth skeletons at The Mammoth Site of Hot Springs, South Dakota. Using bones, fossils, and other evidence, experts are able to piece together a picture of what mammoths looked like and how they lived.

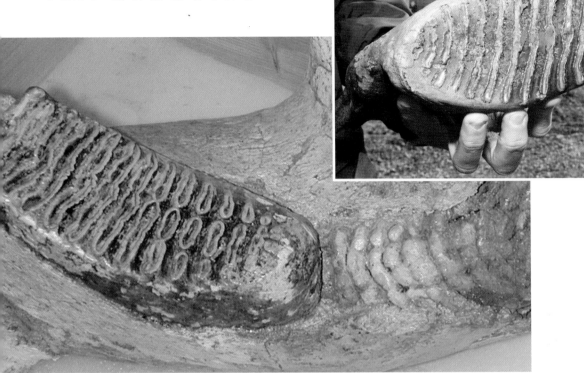

(Above left) *This set of mammoth teeth shows a new molar in the process of pushing out and replacing the old molar. By comparing the size of this mammoth molar* (above right) *with a human hand, you get the sense of its enormous size.*

The structure of the mammoth's teeth helped it grind tough grasses. Enamel ridges on the upper and lower teeth cut past each other as the mammoth moved its jaw back and forth. As the chewing surface of a mammoth's exposed teeth wore down, the molars were pushed out from the jaw by the new molars growing underneath, exposing more chewing surface of the old molars. This made them wear longer. When the mammoth's sixth and last set of molars wore out, the animal could no longer chew. Eventually, it died of starvation.

In addition to six sets of molars, a mammoth also had enormous incisors—the tusks. The world's largest mammoth tusk, found in Texas, measures 16 feet (4.9 meters) in length and came from a Columbian mammoth. The world-record woolly mammoth tusk is just over 13.5 feet (4.11 meters) long, and some tusks weigh 225 pounds (more than 100 kilograms). On the average, however, the tusks of an adult male Columbian mammoth grew to about 10 feet (3 meters) in length and weighed about 115 pounds (52.2 kilograms). A mammoth had

A pair of entwined woolly mammoth tusks is tied to a sled for transport across the Siberian tundra. The distinct nature of the curved tusks is typical of woolly and Columbian mammoth tusks.

two sets of tusks in its lifetime. The first set of tiny "milk tusks" were only a couple of inches (about 5 centimeters) long and erupted when the mammoth was just six months old. About a year later, these baby tusks were replaced by permanent tusks.

Both male and female mammoths had tusks. Male tusks typically were longer and bigger around than female tusks. The tusks consisted of ivory cones that grew continuously out of sockets in the mammoth's skull—sort of like a series of stacked ice-cream cones. The tusks grew between 1 and 6 inches (2 and 15 centimeters) every year. The rate of growth slowed as the animal aged.

Unlike the tusks of modern elephants, mammoth tusks had a distinctive twist because the ivory cones spiraled as they grew. The mammoth tusks grew down from the skull and then curved up and out before turning inward again, occasionally crisscrossing each other at the tips.

A cross section of a mammoth tusk reveals concentric circles. Each circle represents a new growth cone. Scientists can learn a great deal about a mammoth's life by studying the growth patterns in the tusks.

Using their tusks and trunks as weapons, two Columbian mammoths fight to establish dominance.

The hefty tusks served as powerful weapons. The male mammoth used them to grapple with other males for food or to fight over mating partners. They wielded their tusks to intimidate predators, such as the saber-toothed cat. Mammoths also used their tusks on a daily basis to lift heavy objects, scrape bark off trees, and plow snow so that they could reach buried grasses and plants. Because they were used so much, a mammoth's tusks often showed signs of wear and tear. Mammoths frequently chipped or broke their tusks.

Teeth Reveal Age

Knowing that a mammoth could grow up to six sets of teeth during its lifetime helps scientists determine the age of the remains they find. Because each set of molars was larger than the previous one, researchers can estimate an animal's approximate age by measuring the length, width, and depth of its teeth. The amount of exposed replacement molar also helps pinpoint the age of a mammoth, as does the degree of wear and tear on the surface of the extant molars.

A mammoth's first tooth, already visible at birth, was only about 0.5 inch (13 millimeters) long—no bigger than a human molar. At about age two-and-a-half, the mammoth got its second set of molars. By age ten, the mammoth had its third set. The fourth set arrived by age thirteen, the fifth by age twenty-seven, and the last molars—measuring at least 12 inches (30 centimeters) long and weighing 4 pounds (nearly 2 kilograms)—came in around age forty.

Larry Agenbroad measures a set of mammoth molars. This is one method used to determine the animal's age.

[A MAMMOTH'S TRUNK

Before a mammoth could chew its food, it had to lift the plant material to its mouth. For this job, a mammoth used its agile trunk. The trunk was strong enough to yank vegetation out of the ground and long enough to reach up and strip leaves from trees.

The mammoth's trunk was just a very long nose. The animal's nostrils extended from the tip of the trunk to the head. Although the trunk contained no bones or cartilage, it had tens of thousands of muscles that allowed the mammoth to extend and contract its trunk, and to move it in any direction.

In the remains of this mammoth skull and tusks, notice the lack of a trunk. A mammoth's trunk had no bone structure. Instead, it contained thousands of muscles, giving the trunk a full range of mobility.

A thirsty African elephant uses its trunk to get a drink. Like modern elephants, mammoths could use their trunks in a variety of ways.

Projections on the tip of the mammoth's trunk worked like a hand wearing a mitten. With its trunk, the mammoth could perform such delicate maneuvers as plucking tiny flowers from the ground. The mammoth also used its trunk to siphon up to 50 gallons (200 liters) of water into its mouth each day. The trunk could hold about 2.3 gallons (8.5 liters) of water at a time.

In addition to its importance in eating and drinking, the mammoth's trunk was essential for smelling, touching, and communication. A mammoth's sense of smell—like a modern elephant's—was more highly developed than its eyesight. Its trunk enabled the mammoth to distinguish the many scents in its surroundings. Its trunk detected food, water, members of its herd, and other animals. It could detect scent signals given off by another mammoth ready to mate. It even sniffed out danger.

A mammoth probably cuddled members of its group with its trunk and interlocked trunks in a display of greeting or affection, or during a friendly tussle. Like modern elephants, mammoths probably produced sounds—such as a high-pitched, angry trumpeting—by forcing air out of their trunks.

A mammoth also may have used its trunk occasionally to heave large objects out of the way or to strike out at another mammoth. However, it probably took care to protect such a vital and versatile appendage.

Studying the behavior of modern elephants leads scientists to believe that mammoths may have used their trunks to display affection.

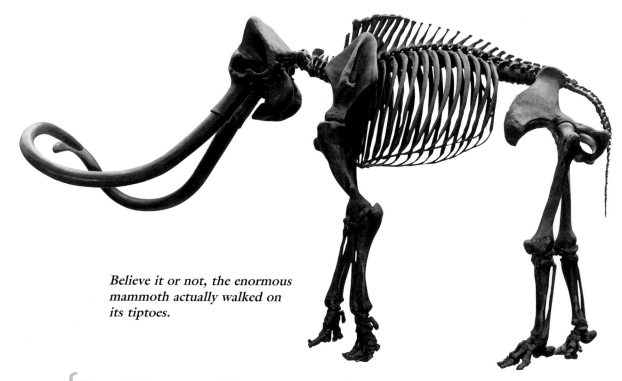

Believe it or not, the enormous mammoth actually walked on its tiptoes.

THE MASSIVE MAMMOTH

With its towering size, massive tusks, and powerful trunk, a healthy adult mammoth had relatively little to fear from predators. The mammoth was indeed king of the Pleistocene. Columbian mammoth males stood up to 13 feet (4 meters) high at the shoulder and weighed in at 10 tons (9 metric tons). Adult male woolly mammoths were smaller. They stood between 9 and 11 feet (about 3 meters) tall and weighed about 6 tons (5 metric tons).

Considering that a mammoth's immense size and bulk were supported by stumplike legs, it's hard to believe this animal walked slightly tiptoed. How was this possible? A mammoth had a tough, spongy pad behind its foot bones. This flexible, springy pad absorbed the animal's weight, cushioned its feet, and gave the mammoth balance and agility as it walked across rugged and steep terrain.

Mammoths were somewhat larger than modern elephants, and their bones were thicker and heavier to better support the animals' greater bulk. Nevertheless, a mammoth could probably run as fast as a modern elephant, whose top speed is about 24 miles (39 kilometers) per hour.

A MAMMOTH'S LIFE

Like elephants, mammoths must have been very sociable animals and probably lived in a matriarchal society, which means that family groups were led by adult females. Modern elephant family groups number from three to twenty or more animals

A group of African elephants forms a definite social structure.
Scientists believe that mammoths behaved in much the same way.

and include the dominant female (the matriarch), her female relatives, and their young. If a mother elephant dies, another female in the group will care for her young.

When young males reach maturity at age ten to fifteen, they are cast out of the family group. Adult male elephants live alone or in small groups with other males. They interact directly with females only during mating, although males and females also may feed and drink together at certain times of the year.

Like modern elephants, a female mammoth carried her baby in her womb for twenty-two months and gave birth every four to eight years—depending on how much food was available and her general health. A female mammoth could have five to six calves during her lifetime. The life expectancy of a woolly mammoth was more than sixty years. The larger Columbian mammoth might have lived to be seventy-five or eighty years old.

COMPARING MAMMOTH SPECIES

Although Columbian and woolly mammoths had similar physiques and behaviors, the two species were different in many ways—primarily because they lived in very different habitats. The Columbian mammoth inhabited low-latitude, temperate grasslands, while the woolly mammoth lived on the cold arctic steppes.

One of the most striking differences was the hairy coat that gave the woolly mammoth its name. The woolly mammoth's coat consisted of three layers of hair and fur. The outer guard hairs were coarse and just over 3 feet (90 centimeters) long. These guard hairs covered an underfur that was thinner and shorter—about 10 to 12 inches (25 to 30 centimeters) long. This underfur covered a thick layer of wool that was roughly

A museum worker inspects a replica of a woolly mammoth. The woolly mammoth's thick coat of hair helped it survive in a much colder climate than the climate in which the Columbian mammoth lived.

1 to 3 inches (2 to 8 centimeters) long. The underfur and wool were densely packed and provided a layer of insulation. Hair and fur covered the woolly mammoth from head to toe, including the trunk. It is likely that the woolly mammoth shed much of its heavy coat in the spring.

A close look at woolly mammoth fur reveals three layers of fur: coarse guard hairs up to 3 feet (1 meter) long; shorter, finer body hair about 12 inches (30 centimeters) long; and a fleecy wool undercoat. The fur kept in body heat while protecting the mammoth from rain, sleet, snow, and cold temperatures.

Most preserved mammoth-fur specimens are orange, yellow, blond, brown, or black in color. In all probability, however, the mammoth fur was originally dark brown or black, but lost some of its color during the thousands of years it lay buried.

Not much is known about the amount of hair on the Columbian mammoth of North America. However, it's safe to assume that it was not hairless because modern African and Asian elephants have sparsely distributed hair over most of their bodies.

In addition to its hairy overcoat, the woolly mammoth had a layer of fat beneath its skin that was 3 to 4 inches (8 to 10 centimeters) thick in places. This probably provided extra insulation from the animal's cold environment.

The woolly mammoth had smaller ears and a shorter tail than its Columbian cousin, which reduced heat loss from those extremities. The Columbian mammoth's larger ears and longer tail increased heat loss to keep the animal cool in its warmer habitat. Likewise, modern-day elephants have larger ears and tails than the woolly mammoth had.

Chapter Four

BONES TELL TALES

We'll never really know what dinosaurs looked like or how they lived. Dinosaur fossils are relatively rare, and fossil hunters almost never find skin or flesh with the bones. In addition, modern reptiles are so different from their extinct relatives that it's hard to make comparisons. The story is different for mammoths, however. Their remains are plentiful, and frozen specimens often include skin, hair, and internal organs. Because their surviving relatives, the elephants, are so closely related, scientists can faithfully reconstruct their appearance—and even their life history.

THE MAMMOTH SITE OF HOT SPRINGS, SOUTH DAKOTA

The largest collection of Columbian mammoth bones in the world is in Hot Springs, South Dakota. So far, forty-nine Columbian mammoths and three woolly mammoths have been dug out of a sinkhole—a sunken area of land—that was filled in by erosion. Researchers predict that at least fifty more mammoths may still lie buried in the deepest portion of the Hot Springs sinkhole. The sinkhole measures 150 feet (46 meters) across and is probably 65 feet (20 meters) deep, but current excavations extend only 25 feet (7.6 meters) down.

The ground at The Mammoth Site of Hot Springs reveals the tusks, teeth, ribs, and skulls of more than four dozen mammoths. These bones hold many clues that help experts piece together how mammoths lived.

Radiocarbon dating of the mammoth bones reveals that the Ice-Age proboscideans died about twenty-six thousand years ago. However, the fifty-two mammoths found at Hot Springs didn't all die at the same time. The mammoths became trapped in the sinkhole over a three-hundred- to seven-hundred-year period.

Twenty-six thousand years ago, the sinkhole at Hot Springs was filled with water that approached 95 degrees Fahrenheit (35 degrees Celsius). It was one of several pools fed by the underground warm-water springs that gave Hot Springs its name. The mammoths' favorite grasses and plants thrived year-round near the warm springs.

Tour guides at the Mammoth Site joke that the Ice-Age sinkhole must have looked like a "giant hot tub surrounded by an all-you-can-eat salad bar" to the mammoths. However, this enticing watering hole proved to be a death trap for many animals.

As mammoths probed the pond's edge for vegetation and water, some of the massive animals accidentally slipped in. Other mammoths willingly ventured into the pool to take a drink or to wash themselves. It didn't take long for the giant creatures to realize that they couldn't climb up the steep, slippery clay banks to get out. Some became frantic and drowned. The rest starved to death.

The first mammoths that died in the watering hole were buried by mud and sand. Others came and they, too, died and were buried above those who preceded them. This went on for three hundred to seven hundred years until the sinkhole filled with dirt—a deep grave for the mammoths. Besides mammoths, the sinkhole trapped twenty-eight other animals, including a giant short-faced bear that may have been lured into the sinkhole to feast on a dying mammoth.

The History of a Sinkhole

The watering hole (in modern-day Hot Springs, South Dakota) that attracted the mammoths was inside a sinkhole. Both were created by the collapse of an underground cavern. When the cavern caved in, the ground above it sank in funnel-type fashion—thus the name *sinkhole*. An underground spring partially filled the sinkhole with water. Mammoths that perished in the sinkhole were buried by sediments that the Jacuzzi-like spring churned and redistributed.

Eventually the spring stopped flowing, and the layers of sediment formed a hard, protective shroud around the animal remains. Over time, erosion wore down the earth surrounding the sinkhole, but the solidified sediments resisted wear and tear. As a result, the sinkhole sediments formed a small hill above the surrounding ground.

This mammoth mausoleum went unnoticed for thousands of years, but it was discovered accidentally in 1974 when the "hill" was partially leveled so that a housing development could be built. Many mammoth bones have been destroyed during other construction projects, but the bulldozer operator who discovered these bones and the contractor he worked for called a paleontologist right away. The scientist immediately recognized the site's value. The contractor halted the housing project, allowing further exploration and development of The Mammoth Site of Hot Springs, South Dakota.

A gurgling spring emerges from the floor of a sinkhole.

So far, all the mammoths that have been found in the sink-hole are males. Most of these animals were in the prime of life—between the ages of thirteen and twenty-nine. These "teenage" and young adult male mammoths were most likely living on their own, having been pushed out of their matriarchal family groups. Like humans their age, the mammoths were curious and adventuresome. With no older female guardians to steer them clear of danger, they wandered into trouble when they got too close to the sinkhole.

In addition to the many skulls, bones, teeth, and tusks that litter the excavated sinkhole, virtually intact skeletons rest in the exact position in which the animals died or were buried. One specimen was found with its delicate hyoid bones, or tongue-support bones, still in place. Also preserved with the skeleton were bile stones, similar to human kidney stones—only much larger.

At the opposite end of the sinkhole, another skeleton paints a tragic picture of a mammoth trying to escape the death trap. His forelegs are stretched outward toward the edge of the sink-hole, and his hind legs are extended backward in a desperate attempt to climb the sinkhole's slippery bank.

The woolly mammoth remains found in the sinkhole include teeth and partial skulls. They were discovered higher up in the sinkhole deposits, suggesting that these animals may have arrived later, when the climate cooled, and some of the Columbian mammoths had begun to migrate to a warmer environment farther south.

Besides mammoths and the giant short-faced bear, the sinkhole has yielded bones from a coyote, a wolf, a camel, a llama, a vulture, a vole, a pocket gopher, a kangaroo rat, a squirrel, and a fish, as well as mollusk shells. The smaller

A helpless mammoth tries to escape from a sinkhole.

animals are important because they reveal more than the mammoths about what the environment of Hot Springs was like twenty-six thousand years ago. For example, the mollusks found at the Mammoth Site tell scientists that the sinkhole did not totally freeze during winter.

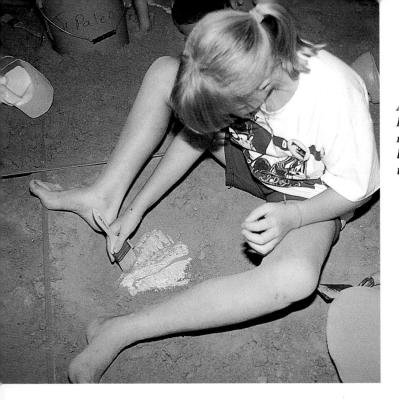

At the Mammoth Site, kids can uncover replicas of mammoth bones buried tens of thousands of years ago.

The ancient burial ground holds other clues about the Hot Springs environment. Pollen samples suggest that the area surrounding Hot Springs was a steppe-tundra—a cold, treeless grassland with shrubby brush, water-rooted plants, sedges, and green grass that flourished even in winter. Today, Hot Springs is a pine-forest and grassland environment.

New finds turn up each year at the Mammoth Site, which is a natural national landmark with a research laboratory and a visitors' center. People who visit in the summer can watch excavation in action.

LA BREA TAR PITS

At the Rancho La Brea Tar Pits in downtown Los Angeles, California, ancient asphalt—a black, sticky material—trapped hundreds of Ice-Age animals, including Columbian mammoths. Before animal remains were discovered in the tar pits, the *brea* (Spanish for "tar") proved most useful to some of the earliest human inhabitants of southern California. Some nine thousand to ten thousand years ago, the predecessors of the Chumash and Gabrielino Indians used the asphalt as an adhesive. It was perfect for repairing tools, sticking decorative shells onto handiwork, and waterproofing baskets and canoes.

Workers excavate Pit 91 at the La Brea Tar Pits in Los Angeles. The skeletons have been preserved in the sticky tar for twenty-eight thousand years.

Later the tar pits were mined for asphalt used in road building. That mining suddenly halted in the late 1800s when ancient bones and other remains were discovered in the tar. Since that time, more than 140 species of plants and 420 species of animals have been extracted from the tar.

Some twenty-five thousand to thirty thousand years ago, certain parts of what is now Los Angeles were covered with

Workers in the early 1900s excavate bones from the tar pits for exhibition. Dr. James Z. Gilbert began the first controlled excavation of the La Brea Tar Pits in 1909. Before that, collectors and amateur paleontologists extracted fossils from the tar pits.

Saber-toothed cats are among the fiercest creatures whose bones have been found in the La Brea Tar Pits.

shallow puddles of gooey tar that were camouflaged by leaves and other debris. When unsuspecting mammoths stepped into these asphalt traps, the tar stuck to their feet and legs like gum to a shoe. Their struggles were futile, and exhaustion eventually claimed their lives.

While many mammoths, mastodons, and other plant eaters have been recovered from the tar pits, most of the bones in the ancient asphalt came from carnivores—meat-eating animals like dire wolves, coyotes, and saber-toothed cats. These predators apparently came to feed on the mammoths and other animals stuck in the thick, gluelike tar. They, too, became trapped.

The tar pits also contain the remains of smaller animals, such as insects and birds. Most of these remains are between

*The asphalt turned bones and teeth in the La Brea pits into black,
rock-hard remains, keeping them extremely well preserved.*

forty thousand and ten thousand years old. The tar pits even revealed the skeletal remains of a woman who lived nine thousand years ago.

All told, about 100 tons (90 metric tons) of material have been salvaged from the tar pits, but very few complete skeletons have been recovered. That's because the asphalt liquefies in hot weather and the buried bones move around.

Bones and teeth are all that's left of the Ice-Age animals at La Brea. Bacteria destroyed all the tissues of the animals, but the asphalt seeped into the hard body parts and preserved them as hard, shiny, black remains.

BONES ABOUND

In addition to the mammoth remains found in the natural traps at Hot Springs and La Brea, thousands of bones litter the continents of Europe, Asia, and North America. One of the largest accumulations of mammoth bones, excavated between 1970 and 1980, is on the Berelekh River in northeastern Siberia. More than eight thousand bones from at least 156 woolly mammoths have been washed out of nearby hills of permafrost

The shoreline of the Berelekh River in Siberia is littered with mammoth bones from more than 150 mammoths.

and dumped along the riverbed. The specimens range from 12,240 to 13,700 years old. During that time, individual mammoths must have become stuck in mud or slipped through the ice and drowned.

Farther downstream, tusk fragments from the site were found along with human Stone Age tools. On one piece of tusk, some ancient artist had carved a mammoth with greatly stretched legs. Although these early humans surely used mammoth bones and tusks as tools, they most likely did not hunt

In 1997 this paleontologist pulled a 12,500-year-old mammoth pelvic bone from the bottom of the Aucilla River in northern Florida. Skeletal remains found underwater are not unusual. In some cases, bones have been washed into rivers. In others, sea levels rose, covering the sites where animals may have died.

the mammoths because the bones are a few thousand years older than the Stone Age site.

On the opposite end of Russia, about 250 miles (400 kilometers) south of Moscow, another concentration of bones was uncovered in 1988. Excavation of the site, known as Sevsk, along the Seva River turned up some four thousand bone specimens from at least thirty-five small woolly mammoths that perished over a short period of time about fourteen thousand years ago.

The Seva River region was once a marshy river floodplain, and it's possible that the mammoths were trapped by flooding, died, and were then quickly buried. The rapid burial would explain why so many skeletal parts were recovered intact. Seven nearly complete skeletons, including those of three calves, were discovered at the site. Perhaps these seven mammoths belonged to the same herd, or even the same family.

Mammoth bones are often found underwater. Remains of many Ice-Age animals—including the bones of an ancestral mammoth and a mastodon—have been fished out of the North Sea. During the ice ages, when sea level fell, the North Sea became dry land. Some mammoths died there. River and lake deposits buried the bones, which then became submerged as sea level rose again during a warmer interglacial period.

Chapter Five

BONES ARE JUST THE BEGINNING

While The Mammoth Site of Hot Springs, the Rancho La Brea Tar Pits, and the depths of the North Sea provide ample skeletal remains of mammoths, the canyon country of the American Southwest offers evidence of an entirely different sort. Two caves in southern Utah contain large quantities of mammoth dung. The dry southwestern climate and the shelter of the caves have preserved these rare specimens for thousands of years. Dung deposits are significant because they tell scientists what the mammoths were eating as well as what vegetation was growing in the area when the animals were alive. Knowing the kinds of plants that existed in the area helps scientists reconstruct the mammoth's Ice-Age climate and environment.

INSIDE BECHAN CAVE

Bechan Cave, named for a Navajo Indian word meaning "big feces," is hollowed out of an ancient sand dune preserved as sandstone. It is 100 feet (30 meters) across, 30 feet (9 meters) high, and 170 feet (52 meters) from the entrance to the rear. Just beneath the cave floor is a blanket of dung 16 inches (41 centimeters) thick. It is the largest dung deposit in North America.

Mammoth dung helps scientists learn what kinds of plants mammoths ate. This information gives clues about the climate and environment in places where mammoths lived.

Bechan Cave (above) *in the southwestern United States is an excellent source of ancient dung. The cave contains the dung of shrub oxen* (left), *mammoths, and other extinct animals.*

Besides Columbian mammoth dung, Bechan Cave contains the dung of shrub oxen (the southern cousins of the arctic musk oxen), horses, bison, mountain goats, and Shasta ground sloths. The cave also contains hair from several of these animals.

The Columbian mammoth dung in the cave dates from 13,500 years to 11,670 years ago—less than seven hundred years before the global extinction of the species. The dung, therefore, reveals the diet of the mammoths in the last centuries of their existence.

The mammoth dung contains about 90 percent grass mixed with sedges, spruce, sagebrush, and willow. These plants are characteristic of a subalpine climate, not the desert environment found at Bechan Cave in modern times. So the plant remains in the dung tell us that 11,670 years ago, this part of southern Utah was much cooler and wetter than it is these days.

Scientists can reconstruct the Bechan Cave environment even farther back in time—up to forty thousand years ago—with the help of another creature. The bushy-tailed pack rat lived in the area during the Pleistocene and continues to inhabit the region. This pack rat is a collector that picks up twigs, branches, plants, and other items and stockpiles them in its den in a heap called a midden. Pack-rat urine, which contains resin from the conifer

(Inset) *Researchers can reconstruct the Columbian mammoth's habitat by examining a pack-rat midden* (above) *found near Bechan Cave.*

trees it munches on, cements the midden. When rock-hard middens are preserved in caves and alcoves, they become time capsules of past environments.

[A LOOK AT COWBOY CAVE

Cowboy Cave in Utah also contains an ancient bed of dung. It consists mostly of bison dung but includes plant fragments too

The cave fill in Cowboy Cave, Utah, contained the dung of bison, shrub oxen, and mammoths. The dung bed, found below levels where human remains were found, dates back to thirteen thousand years ago.

large for a bison to have passed. The size of the plant fragments and the discovery of a broken tusk tip suggest that mammoths also visited the cave. The dung bed in Cowboy Cave dates back eleven thousand to thirteen thousand years, making it about the same age as the one in nearby Bechan Cave. The dung suggests that the Ice-Age environment around Cowboy Cave was probably lush grassland.

The evidence from southern Utah has allowed scientists to reconstruct the region's environment from 40,000 years ago up to 11,670 years ago—the final days of the Columbian mammoth. This period is also significant because it marks the closing years of the ice ages and the arrival of prehistoric human cultures in the Americas. In fact, mammoths and other four-legged animals were not the only visitors to Bechan Cave and Cowboy Cave. Overlying the dung beds is charcoal from fires lit by people seeking refuge in the caves between 8,700 and 550 years ago. These cave deposits allow scientists to make useful comparisons. For example, they can compare the diets of mammoths that lived in the American Southwest to the stomach contents of frozen mammoths that lived in the arctic permafrost region.

FROZEN MAMMOTHS

The most complete mammoths ever found are the woolly mammoths preserved in nature's deep freeze—the permafrost of the arctic. Permafrost is ground that is frozen up to 1,500 feet (460 meters) deep. Some of the most impressive woolly mammoth finds have been unearthed from the permafrost of Siberia. Most of the preserved mammoth carcasses come from two time periods—before thirty thousand years ago and between thirteen thousand and ten thousand years ago. These were interglacials. The slightly warmer climate during these periods may have caused an increase in water runoff resulting in mudflows that buried the mammoths quickly. The buildup of ice in the sediments around the bodies would have preserved the dead mammoths.

During the more recent interglacial period, members of native groups living in Siberia and Alaska occasionally found frozen mammoths. According to Siberian and Inuit legends that have survived through generations of oral traditions, these native peoples believed that mammoths were living creatures that spent all their time underground. If the animals came to the surface, they died immediately. Siberian legends also claimed that misfortune, or even death, befell anyone who disturbed a mammoth.

THE FIRST FROZEN MAMMOTH

In 1799 a Siberian ivory trader and hunter noticed a partially entombed carcass of a mammoth that had been lodged in ice at the mouth of the Lena River. Ignoring the omen of doom, the hunter cut off the animal's tusks and sold them when the mammoth became totally dislodged from the earth in 1803.

Mikhail Adams of the Russian Academy of Sciences heard about the mammoth and visited the site in 1806. By then only the animal's skeleton remained. The flesh had decomposed and been scavenged by animals. Tribal people living nearby had even fed some of the flesh to their dogs.

Still, Adams was excited. The skeleton was almost entirely intact—only one foreleg was missing. Adams was also able to retrieve samples of the mammoth's skin and hair. Next he tracked down the animal's tusks and purchased them. In 1808 the mammoth's remains were transported to St. Petersburg, Russia, and reconstructed. It was the first mammoth skeleton ever to be mounted.

In the early nineteenth century, British geologist Charles Lyell proposed that the woolly mammoth was really an elephant that had been displaced from its home in central Asia, where elephant herds abounded. He believed the animal had died in the great biblical flood, and the floodwaters had transported the carcass to Siberia. According to Lyell, the flood explained why the skeleton was found in a place where there were no living elephants.

French anatomist Georges Cuvier had a different idea. He believed that mammoths were distinct from living elephants and were adapted to cold climates. Cuvier argued that raging floodwaters would have destroyed the carcass. He noted that neither the frozen mammoth carcass nor the bones showed any of the wear and tear that would result from being tossed and tumbled in a flood. Cuvier suggested that the mammoth was an extinct species—a radical notion at a time when few people believed in extinction.

THE BERESOVKA MAMMOTH

In 1901 Otto Herz and Eugen Pfizenmayer of the Russian Academy of Sciences undertook one of the most arduous mammoth expeditions ever. They led an 11,000-mile (18,000-kilometer), ten-month journey from St. Petersburg to Beresovka in northeastern Siberia. The scientists made the round trip by train, boat, sleigh, foot, and horseback—enduring temperatures as low as minus 54 degrees Fahrenheit (minus 48 degrees Celsius).

The object of their pursuit was a mammoth originally found by a local hunter. The decomposing mammoth turned out to

Otto Herz and Eugen Pfizenmayer stand with what would come to be called the Beresovka mammoth, uncovered during a 1901 expedition.

be a thirty-five- to forty-year-old male that died in a landslide about thirty thousand years ago. Its numerous broken bones, wrenched vertebrae, and blood clots indicated that the mammoth had died instantly. The mammoth even had food between its teeth—attesting to its sudden death.

The expedition members cut the carcass into pieces so that the massive creature could be extracted from the still-frozen ground. They then built a log cabin heated by stoves to thaw the body parts. The dismembered Beresovka mammoth was transported to St. Petersburg, where it was reassembled and displayed for Tsar Nicholas II and his wife, Alexandra.

MORE MYSTERIOUS MAMMOTHS

In 1948 geologists working on Siberia's Taimyr Peninsula found another frozen mammoth. It was a small, fifty- to fifty-five-year-old male with some tissue, skin, and hair still attached. The skeleton, dating back 11,500 years, was complete, except for a few bones from the toes and tail.

In 1972 another male mammoth was recovered from the bank of the Shandrin River in Siberia. This find was significant because it yielded previously unknown information about the abdominal cavity of a mammoth, including the stomach and intestines.

A fifty-year-old male mammoth was found on a small tributary of Siberia's Khatanga River in 1977. Although badly scavenged and decomposed, the remains included some skin from the head, parts of the trunk, two feet, and the entire left ear. The mammoth's ear was less than one-fifth the size of the ear of an African elephant of the same age and gender.

REMAINS OF BABY MAMMOTHS

Although countless bones, teeth, and tusks have been found in Alaska, very few frozen woolly mammoths have been found in the permafrost there. The most significant find was made near Fairbanks in 1948. That's when the partial head, trunk, and foreleg of a baby mammoth, nicknamed Effie, were discovered. This calf dates back 21,300 years and would have weighed about 200 pounds (100 kilograms) when alive.

Mammoth Mummies

The word *mummy* probably brings to mind the preserved human remains of ancient Egyptians. However, frozen mammoths buried in permafrost also qualify as mummies. Although the mummification processes are different, frozen mammoths share a distinct similarity with Egyptian mummies. Both processes rely on the desiccation, or drying out, of the corpse.

Ancient Egyptians believed in an afterlife. They took great care to preserve the bodies of the dead for their life after death. First, they removed all the internal organs—except the heart—and preserved each one in a separate jar. Then they placed the body in a bed of salts to draw all the moisture out of the corpse. Finally, the Egyptians stuffed the dried corpse with sawdust and linen and wrapped it in linen strips and a shroud.

Mammoth mummies are the result of natural processes. When a dead mammoth is covered with a layer of permafrost, moisture from its body is not released into the atmosphere. Instead, it crystallizes and becomes part of the overlying permafrost. Over time, more and more of the body's moisture is transformed into ice crystals. Eventually, the mammoth carcass dehydrates, shrivels, and becomes mummified.

In this illustration, seal hunters discover a well-preserved mammoth frozen in the ice of the Yamal Peninsula, Siberia.

While most of the mammoth remains have been male, a female calf was discovered on Siberia's Yamal Peninsula in 1988. The calf, named Mascha by scientists, was only three to four months old when she died. A deep wound on the back of her right hind foot may have been the cause of death.

Perhaps the most remarkable find to date was the 1977 discovery of a nearly complete baby woolly mammoth in northeastern Siberia. The male calf was exposed as gold miners blasted permafrost with high-pressure water jets. Named Dima for a nearby stream, the calf is the most complete mammoth ever unearthed.

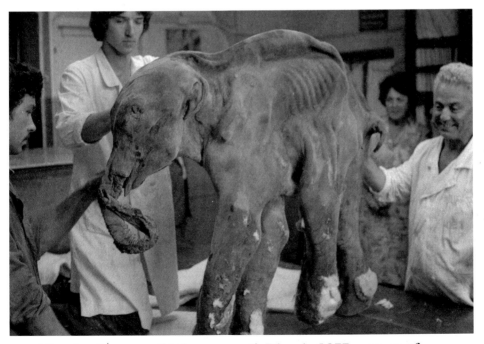

After the discovery of baby mammoth Dima in 1977, a group of excited taxidermists examine the incredibly intact body.

Dima's body, found on a tributary of the Kolyma River, still had its internal organs and traces of hair. Most of the time, soft tissue and hair don't survive.

Dima was less than a year old when he died. He was about 3 feet (90 centimeters) tall and weighed 220 to 250 pounds (100 to 115 kilograms). His mummified carcass was withered because the icy silt in which he was buried had drawn the moisture out of his body. Nonetheless, his small body—including the internal organs—was intact. Even some of his hair still clung to his skin.

Dima was not a healthy calf when he died forty thousand years ago. Examinations of the preserved carcass showed that he lacked the normal layers of fat, and his stomach contained a large number of parasites as well as silt and some of his own hair.

It's hard to say exactly how Dima died. One possible scenario is that the calf became stuck in a mud bog and couldn't free himself. He may have struggled for days, which could have depleted his stored fat. Trapped animals often exhibit delirious behavior, and Dima may have chewed on his own hair as the stress of his dilemma overwhelmed him.

The harder Dima struggled, the deeper he probably sank in the bog until, ultimately, exhaustion or suffocation from the mud and water claimed his last breath. Dima's mother and other females in the group, unable to save him, may have stood vigil, mourning his death. This would explain why Dima's corpse was not mutilated by predators and scavengers. In time, the herd moved on, and mudflows buried the calf deeper, preserving his body for forty thousand years.

Chapter Six

THE HUMAN FACTOR

Ancient cave paintings show that mammoths captured the attention—and perhaps the admiration—of the people who shared the land with them. The most extensive cave paintings and carvings of woolly mammoths are in southern France and Spain. Rouffignac Cave in France contains some of the most impressive Ice-Age mammoth art.

The prehistoric artists used charcoal, minerals, and other natural materials to create black, red, yellow, and even purple pigments. They applied their natural paints to the cave walls with their fingers or tools—maybe brushes made from animal hair or plant fibers. When working on rough surfaces, they may have sprayed the paint through some type of pipe that they held in their mouth. Because the cave was pitch-dark inside, the artists probably used fires and torches to light up the area as they worked. They also filled stone ladles with animal fat and set the fat on fire, creating a sort of prehistoric lantern.

Rouffignac Cave contains more than one hundred mammoth renderings, including detailed engravings and black drawings. One engraving is 31 inches (78 centimeters) tall and 4 feet (1.2 meters) long. Another drawing on a ceiling in the cave is more than 6 feet (2 meters) long. Most of the renderings are side views of individual mammoths. One drawing, however, shows

Ancient humans must have been impressed by mammoths. Prehistoric artists painted images of mammoths on cave walls. This one, found in a cave in France, dates to 20,000 B.C.

two rows of mammoths facing one another. Perhaps the artist had witnessed two groups of mammoths greeting one another after having been separated.

While some depictions show highly stylized mammoths with exaggerated features, many prehistoric cave artists etched or drew mammoths in true-to-life style and in amazing detail. One drawing shows the distinctive mitten-shaped projections on the tip of the mammoth's trunk and accurately portrays how the animal's foot expanded under its weight. In other cave drawings, the artist took care to show the high-domed skull, sloping back, short tail, and hairy coat of the woolly mammoth.

Although cave or rock-shelter depictions of mammoths have been found only in western Europe and the Ural Mountains of Russia, crude mammoth petroglyphs—figures pecked into rock walls—have been discovered on the Colorado Plateau in the American Southwest. Since no woolly mammoth remains have ever been found in the Southwest, it's safe to assume the petroglyphs are likenesses of Columbian mammoths or, perhaps, mastodons—a more primitive proboscidean.

CARVINGS AND SCULPTURES OF MAMMOTHS

While scientists cannot pinpoint exactly when cave paintings and petroglyphs were created, mammoth carvings and sculptures can be dated reliably. Researchers know they were made during the ice ages because they have been found with other human artifacts from that period.

During an excavation of a 12,700-year-old site in Gönnersdorf, Germany, archaeologists—scientists who study prehistoric human cultures—found the largest-known collection of stone and ivory mammoth depictions. The site contained sixty-two mammoth

Larry Agenbroad holds a tiny mammoth figurine carved by ancient humans.

figures carved in stone. The engravings even distinguish between adult and young mammoths, showing the downward sloping back of adults and the domed back of young mammoths.

It is difficult to understand how the people who lived at the site viewed mammoths. Although mammoths are a predominant theme at Gönnersdorf, the site has no evidence suggesting the people hunted or ate mammoths. While the site contains many reindeer bones, there is not a single carving or engraving of a reindeer.

Other mammoth engravings in stone and ivory have been found in France and Siberia. Russia has produced the largest number of three-dimensional mammoth figurines, which were sculpted in clay-rich stone and limestone. Ivory statuettes of mammoths from Germany date back thirty thousand years, making them among the oldest figurines in the world.

The Early Humans

Modern humans originated in Africa about one hundred thousand years ago and migrated through Europe between forty thousand and thirty thousand years ago. This latter group of prehistoric people looked just like us, and they are the ones who created the Ice-Age mammoth art. They lived at the end of the Stone Age—a period of time when people made most of their tools out of stone.

The Stone Age began about 2.5 million years ago, when the earliest humans made the first identifiable stone tools. It lasted through the ice ages and ended when people began making tools from copper, bronze, and iron. The Stone Age ended at different times in different parts of the world. In the Americas, people continued to use stone tools well into the nineteenth century.

BUILDING WITH BONES

When scientists find mammoth bones, teeth, or tusks, they carefully preserve the remains for study or for display in a museum. Several thousand years ago, however, early humans often used mammoth bones in more practical ways. They built hut-type dwellings out of the bones and carved tools and other objects from the animals' ivory tusks.

Throughout the Pleistocene, as mammoths died of old age, disease, or other natural causes, their carcasses and bones were scattered across central and eastern Europe. Hunters also may have left behind the bones of mammoths they killed. In the absence of caves and rock shelters, some enterprising Paleolithic (Stone Age) people used mammoth bones to build huts as protection from the elements. The most impressive were made between thirty thousand and fourteen thousand years ago.

Some seventy mammoth-bone huts—all of which collapsed long ago—have been discovered at about a dozen sites, mostly in Russia. Crude excavating techniques originally led people to believe the mounds of bones were prehistoric garbage dumps— litter left by Ice-Age hunters who stripped the meat off the bones and then tossed them into piles.

Beginning in the 1920s, the bone mounds were excavated more carefully and methodically. Only then was the truth

This reconstructed mammoth-bone hut is similar to huts discovered in Ukraine, the Czech Republic, and Poland. Such remains date to around twenty-seven thousand years ago.

discovered. The ancient builders didn't just haphazardly stack the mammoth bones on top of one another. They used the geometric shapes of the bones to their advantage.

For one dwelling, mammoth skulls were placed in a semi-circle to form a foundation. Atop the skulls, jawbones were arranged chin down in a herringbone pattern to form the upper wall. Walls of other dwellings were constructed from the long leg bones, placed vertically. Still other mammoth-bone huts incorporated shoulder blades, pelvic bones, and other large bones. While the kinds of bones used and their placement varied, all the mammoth-bone huts shared some similarities. They were typically round or oval and measured between 13 and 22 feet (4.0 to 6.7 meters) across. Many had a hearth.

Prehistoric people carefully constructed their dwellings of mammoth bones, sticks, and hides. Five mammoth mandibles (lower jaws) provide a solid foundation and lower wall of this bone hut.

Mammoth tusks may have been used at entrances or as roof supports. Most likely, a bone-framed roof was covered with sod or animal hides that were held down with more large mammoth bones.

Because trees and wood were scarce in the cold climate of the Russian Plain (a region in western Russia), the hut dwellers probably burned fresh bones for warmth and to cook food. Fresh bones, which still contain marrow and fat, burn relatively well and could have been stored in nearby pits where the permafrost would have preserved them. Mammoth hunters also may have stockpiled meat from their kills in these Ice-Age freezers.

While mammoth huts have been discovered around the Russian villages of Borshevo and Kostenki, which got its name from the Russian word for "bonfire" or "bone-fire," the most impressive bone-hut site is at Mezhirich in Ukraine. The site contains at least five dwellings dating back fifteen thousand years. The remains of about 150 mammoths were used to build the huts. Inward-facing skulls, along with pelvic and long bones, formed the foundation of each dwelling. On top of these were more skulls, shoulder blades, pelvic bones, vertebrae, and other bones. Even higher, tusks probably held down animal hides that were stretched over the frame of the hut. Some bones have holes drilled into them. It is possible that pegs were inserted into these holes to hold the bones in position—or perhaps clothing or meat was hung from the pegs.

Building these bone huts was no small feat. After all, mammoth bones are very heavy. A mammoth skull with tusks can weigh more than 300 pounds (140 kilograms). One dwelling at Mezhirich contained about 385 bones with a total weight of 46,300 pounds (21,000 kilograms). Other dwellings were smaller, but archaeologists estimate that it still took between four and six days to build a hut, not including the time it took to collect the bones.

Little is known about how many people lived in the bone huts or how long they occupied them. The abundance of artifacts at some sites suggests that the dwellings were occupied by large groups for long periods of time. At Mezhirich, 4,600 flint artifacts were found scattered around a circular pit beneath the mammoth bones—evidence of toolmaking over an extended period of time.

Scientists have also discovered sites in the region that were built during the same period but do not have mammoth-bone huts. Perhaps the Pleistocene people lived in the bone dwellings during the harsh winters and moved to their less-durable "summer homes" during the warmer months.

Tools, Weapons, and More

Paleolithic people used mammoth bones for more than building materials. At some of the mammoth-bone hut sites, leg bones were found standing upright in the ground. Dents, notches, and other marks on the ends of the bones indicate that they may have been used as anvils, tables, or even as parts of barbecue pits. Foot bones and shoulder blades may have served as anvils or working surfaces. Stone Age people also fashioned paddle-shaped shovels, spatulas, cleavers, digging sticks, and even fishhooks from mammoth bones.

Scientists have discovered mammoth bones with geometric patterns painted on them covering graves. This suggests that the bones may have served some kind of ceremonial, spiritual, or ritual purpose. Burial sites have also yielded examples of the remarkable craftsmanship of Stone Age people.

In Russia the graves of an elderly man and two children contained ivory staffs, daggers, carvings, needles, bracelets, and beads made from mammoth tusks. Some 3,500 beads draped each body in neat rows across the forehead and body, down the arms and legs, and around the ankles. Scientists believe that the beads may have once adorned the clothing in which the people were buried. While the beads still remain, the clothing must have decayed long ago.

Ivory carving was time-consuming, labor-intensive work. Because Ice-Age artisans had only crude stone tools, it probably took about forty-five minutes to make each of the beads found in the Russian graves. After chiseling or splitting pieces of ivory from a mammoth tusk, a sculptor whittled, cut, and engraved the ivory to

The tip of this mammoth tusk was intricately carved by an artist about twenty-seven thousand years ago.

Ancient people used mammoth ivory to carve figurines. This head, found in the Czech Republic, was carved more than twenty-four thousand years ago.

produce beads or figurines. Prehistoric artisans also fashioned tools, utensils, and weapons, often engraving a crisscross pattern on the handles to provide a firm grip. Early humans made ivory harpoons, sewing needles, and combs, too.

Considering how rock-hard ivory is, it's remarkable that Ice-Age people were able to make straight spears out of curved mammoth tusks. Hunters or craftspeople may have soaked the tusks in liquid for a long time and then heated them just enough to soften the ivory and change its shape.

A similar technique may have been used to make the world's oldest boomerang. The twenty-thousand-year-old weapon was found in a cave in Poland. The boomerang was thrown not with the intention of its returning to the thrower, but to strike and, hopefully, kill an animal. The weapon's shape follows the natural curvature of a mammoth's tusk, and each end has thin, tapered edges like a bird's wing.

Stone Age people were indeed master carvers of ivory. Some of their most impressive works were ivory statuettes and figurines. One of the oldest of these three-dimensional carvings depicts a horse and was carved with stone tools about thirty thousand years ago.

Most Ice-Age ivory carvings of humans represent women. These so-called Venus figurines (fertility figures) often greatly exaggerate the female body with a stomach, breasts, and buttocks that are larger than normal. Few of the figurines show facial details, such as nostrils, a mouth, or eyebrows. Typically the arms are close to the body, resting on the stomach or breasts. Most of the ivory Venus figurines have been found in central and eastern Europe and Siberia.

Unlike most of the faceless Venus figurines, one twenty-three-thousand-year-old carving found in Siberia depicts hair, eyes, nose, and mouth. Hers is the face of a people who lived among the mammoths—but while her people thrived and evolved, the great mammoths faded from existence.

Chapter Seven

THEN THERE WERE NONE

Why did mammoths disappear from Earth? This question remains one of the great unsolved mysteries of all time. Despite everything scientists have learned about these animals, they do not know why the Columbian mammoth and the woolly mammoth died out at about the same time—roughly ten thousand to eleven thousand years ago.

Extinctions are not unusual. Throughout time, thousands of kinds of plants, animals, and other living things have been replaced by species that were better suited to their environment. Look at proboscidean evolution, for example. First there was the hippolike *Moeritherium*, which was followed by *Deinotherium* and then *Loxodonta*, *Elephas*, and *Mammuthus*. Each of these animals had features that made it better able to survive than its predecessors.

The extinction of mammoths was different. Mammoths were not replaced by a better-adapted species that was competing for the same habitat—and it wasn't just mammoths that disappeared so mysteriously. Between forty thousand and ten thousand years ago, many of Earth's largest mammals vanished. In North America, 70 percent of the mammals weighing more than 100 pounds (over 40 kilograms) disappeared during that time period. In all, about one hundred species of large animals

Scientists are still working to find out why mammoths died out ten thousand to eleven thousand years ago. There are two main theories— overhunting and climate change.

This illustration includes many of the animals that lived during the Pleistocene epoch. Can you spot giant ground sloths, ancient bison, dire wolves, and early horses?

became extinct. These included mastodons, several species of horses and camels, giant ground sloths, deer, giant stags, saber-toothed cats, dire wolves, shrub oxen, giant beavers, four-horned antelope, giant peccaries, and tapirs.

The extinctions were not limited to North America. In Eurasia, the giant deer, cave bear, and woolly rhinoceros joined the woolly mammoth on the extinction list. In South America, the gomphotheres, native species of horses and armadillos, and giant rodents perished. Australia lost 90 percent of its large animals, including giant kangaroos and wombats.

Extinction reverberated across all the continents except Antarctica during the Late Pleistocene. Africa, Australia, and Asia were struck first, followed by Europe and the Americas. Australia and the Americas were hit hardest.

While extinction claimed many large animals forty thousand to ten thousand years ago, smaller animals and much of Earth's marine and aquatic life fared just fine. That's because extinction hits larger animals harder. A habitat can support more small animals than large ones. Consequently, big animals are more likely to be totally wiped out.

In addition, larger animals have fewer young. For example, mammoths did not reproduce until they were about fifteen years old. Females were pregnant for almost two years and gave birth to just one calf. Until a calf was six to eight years old and could survive on its own, the female was not able to give birth again. Because a large animal reproduces less often and has fewer young than a smaller animal, it's more difficult for populations of large animals to recover from traumatic events.

What were the traumatic events that caused the extinction of the world's largest land mammals? There are two major theories:

1. According to the overkill theory, mammoths and other large animals were annihilated by human hunters.
2. According to the overchill theory, the world's climate and vegetation changed dramatically at the end of the last Ice Age. Large animals couldn't cope with the resulting changes in their habitats and eventually succumbed.

Which theory is correct? The answer remains to be determined. Then again, maybe extinction can't be attributed to just one cause.

THE OVERKILL THEORY

The overkill theory is based, in large part, on the coincidence between the arrival of Ice-Age hunters in North America about twelve thousand years ago and the disappearance of the mammoths. These Ice-Age hunters, or Paleo-Indians, had followed the same path as the mammoths—traveling from Eurasia across the Bering land bridge into North America.

The circumstantial evidence for the Ice-Age overkill theory is strong. The animals that disappeared were the ones most vulnerable to human predation, and they vanished soon after humans arrived. Why would the Ice-Age hunters obliterate such a valuable food resource? Some scientists think the hunters may have become overspecialized, hunting mammoths almost exclusively. Then, once mammoths became scarce, hunters switched to other animals, such as bison.

Paleo-Indians had few weapons that could bring down a massive, powerful, and potentially dangerous mammoth. Some experts believe that hunters often killed mammoths and other large animals by driving them over a cliff. However, critics point out that mammoths usually lived in herds. They doubt that Paleo-Indians were skilled enough to destroy an entire herd of mammoths and argue that mammoths probably weren't reckless enough to follow one another off the edge of a cliff. They also point out that cliffs were uncommon in most of the areas where mammoths lived.

Instead of large-scale mammoth kills, the hunters may have selected younger mammoths as prey. Their meat was tenderer, and the youngsters lacked the experience of adult animals to evade a hunter's pursuit. If this is true, mammoths may have become extinct because youngsters were being killed faster than they could be replaced. After all, an adult female mammoth gave birth to just one calf every six to eight years. As a result, mammoth herds would have become progressively older and smaller until the animals disappeared completely.

One reason scientists do not agree about how—and to what extent—Paleo-Indians hunted mammoths is that they have very

An illustration depicts ancient hunters trying to separate a woolly mammoth from its herd. There are many theories about the predator-prey relationship between mammoths and ancient humans.

little information to work with. They have discovered only a handful of sites that show clear evidence of mammoth kills or butchering. The first site was discovered in Colorado in 1932. Excavations at the site, known as Dent, turned up eleven adolescent and young adult female mammoths, one adult male mammoth, and three spearpoints. Three years later, several spearpoints were found with the remains of six mammoths in Clovis, New Mexico.

Several sites in southern Arizona's San Pedro Valley also offer evidence of Paleo-Indian mammoth hunters. At one locale, called Naco, scientists discovered eight Clovis-style spearpoints with the remains of an adult mammoth. The spearpoints were found in the animal's rib cage and next to the skull, shoulder blade, and vertebrae—areas where spears could have done fatal

The Ice-Age Hunters

Ice-Age hunters entered North America from Eurasia by crossing the same Bering land bridge that the mammoths and other large animals had used earlier. These Paleo-Indians have been divided into two cultures—the Clovis and their descendants, the Folsom.

Clovis and Folsom cultures are distinguished from each other by the types of spear points they used. The Clovis spear point was leaf-shaped with a wide groove, or flute, chipped from the base on both sides. Folsom spear points were slightly smaller, but the fluted portion of the point was much longer—sometimes running the full length of the spear point.

The Clovis spear point was first discovered with mammoth remains, while the Folsom spear point was initially discovered in Folsom, New Mexico, with the remains of extinct bison. As a result, people of the Clovis culture are called mammoth hunters, and people of the Folsom culture are known as bison hunters.

damage. There is no evidence that the animal was butchered. It may have been "the one that got away."

At Lehner Ranch—a site just 2 miles (3 kilometers) from Naco—scientists discovered thirteen Clovis points along with the remains of thirteen young Columbian mammoths that lived about eleven thousand years ago. The excavation also turned up eight stone butchering tools and the remains of a mastodon, a horse, a bison, a tapir, a bear, and a camel.

Just north of Naco and Lehner Ranch, in an area known as Murray Springs, scientists found a grouping of mammoth footprints. At the edge of the grouping, researchers uncovered the partially butchered skeleton of a Columbian mammoth. The footprints might represent the mammoth's last steps, or they may have been left by another mammoth who guarded or mourned a dying companion.

Researchers also found a remarkable tool made from the leg bone of a mammoth. The tool, which looks like a huge, blunt sewing needle, was probably used to straighten wood to make spear shafts. While many similar tools have been found in Eurasia, the Murray Springs mammoth-bone shaft wrench is the only one of its kind ever discovered in North America.

(Left) *Footprints in the earth and a butchered mammoth skeleton have been found at Murray Springs in Arizona, indicating an ancient kill site.* (Above) *Bone shaft wrenches, made from mammoth bones, were used by prehistoric people in Europe and North America.*

Half of the shaft wrench was found in one of the footprint depressions. The other half rested on the rim of the depression. The tool may have dropped from a hunter's belt as he attempted to kill the mammoth, or the hunter may have been trampled in a struggle with the mammoth as he tried to bring down the animal.

Scientists have also unearthed horse, camel, bison, and other mammoth remains at Murray Springs. Half a dozen spear points were also excavated. Stone flakes that fit on the broken spear-point bases from a nearby campsite were found among the animal bones. A stone knife was discovered in a mammoth rib cage, suggesting that Paleo-Indians did butcher the mammoths for meat.

Other sites in North America also offer evidence of humans removing mammoth meat from bones. Chopping tools made from mammoth shoulder blades found at the Lange-Ferguson site in South Dakota suggest that humans butchered one adult mammoth and one juvenile mammoth.

Colby, Wyoming, is another site where parts of half a dozen Columbian mammoths were found in small mounds, along with stone points and a granite chopper. Some researchers have suggested that the Paleo-Indians stacked frozen mammoth meat in piles, surrounded the mounds with ribs and other parts of the carcass, and covered the structures with snow and ice to preserve the choice meat.

Some critics of the overkill theory claim that since scientists have located fewer than a dozen kill sites, it is hard to imagine that humans killed enough mammoths to wipe the animals out completely. They say that if people hunted mammoths to extinction, we should see many more spear points and other hunting and butchering tools at mammoth sites.

According to supporters of the overkill theory, however, the remains found at these sites represent only a tiny percentage of the animals killed by humans. They argue that most mammoth remains were not preserved. Some were scattered by scavengers or by the forces of nature. Others were lost to decay and weathering. Geological conditions would have to be just right to preserve both the mammoth bones and the spear points that killed them.

While evidence of humans hunting mammoths in North America is limited, it's even less apparent in Eurasia. The vast number of bones at the mammoth-bone hut sites in Siberia initially prompted many scientists to believe that early people must have hunted a lot of mammoths, eaten their meat, and then used the leftover bones to build their huts. However, radiocarbon dating has revealed that the age of the bones varied by thousands of years. Thus, the more logical conclusion is that the hut dwellers scrounged the bones of dead mammoths for building materials and tools.

Despite this discouraging discovery, advocates of the overkill theory have not given up. They have asked their critics to explain why the hut dwellers were living on cold, windswept grasslands in the first place. Certainly these people could have lived in less harsh places. Perhaps they lived under such seemingly inhospitable conditions because mammoths and other grazing animals favored the open grasslands. If the survival of these people depended on hunting mammoths, it was clearly the best place for them to live. Advocates also point out that the hut dwellers needed fresh bones to burn as fuel. This is further circumstantial evidence that the Ice-Age people of Eurasia hunted mammoths.

One archaeological investigation in Krakow, Poland, turned up some unusual mammoth remains—nineteen hyoid bones. Cut marks on the bones suggest that early humans feasted on roasted mammoth tongue. Perhaps early people hunted mammoths and took only the usable, easily carried parts of the animal. The tongue may have been considered an Ice-Age delicacy, or it may have been the only source of fat during certain seasons.

Some experts believe that early hunters wiped out mammoths in a blitzkrieg-type offensive. (*Blitzkrieg* is a German word meaning "lightning war," and it defined the swift and violent attacks of the German army during World War II.) According to the blitzkrieg model, when human hunters invaded North America, they found prey that had never been hunted by humans and had no reason to fear the two-legged creatures carrying spears. The hunters struck rapidly, killing the vulnerable animals before they learned to avoid the hunters and their weapons. The ease of hunting meant that the early humans did not have to devise elaborate schemes, such as driving herds off cliffs. Wherever the mammoths went, the humans followed with their blitzkrieg attacks.

In the blitzkrieg model, extinction would have occurred quickly, leaving little archaeological evidence, such as spears and other weapons. The blitzkrieg model also might explain why so few cave paintings and ivory carvings of extinct animals have been found in the Americas. The animals may have been killed off so quickly that people didn't have a chance to paint or carve their likenesses. Supporters of the blitzkrieg model are not surprised that so few mammoth kill sites have been found. What's more surprising, they say, is that any kill sites have been discovered.

Many scientists disagree with the blitzkrieg model. They find it difficult to believe that Stone Age hunters could—or would—have wiped out all the mammoths and many other large animals in less than one thousand years.

THE OVERCHILL THEORY

If humans didn't wipe out the mammoths, what did? Some scientists blame a natural climatic event. "Overchill" is a popular and catchy term to describe this theory, but unfortunately it is also inaccurate. Although the Late Pleistocene extinctions occurred during the ice ages, Earth's climate was actually warming up at that time. The Late Pleistocene was an interglacial period—a time when temperatures were rising and glaciers were melting. So maybe "underchill" rather than "overchill" would more accurately describe the climate change of the Late Pleistocene.

The climate model of extinction suggests that about thirteen thousand years ago, worldwide temperatures increased by as much as 11 degrees Fahrenheit (6 degrees Celsius) within just a decade or two, and moisture and temperature extremes between summer and winter became more pronounced. While summers became much hotter and drier, winters may have been colder and wetter. The change in climate meant a shorter growing season for plants.

To endure, plant species became limited to those habitats where they grew best. As a result, the kinds and diversity of plants in many parts of the world changed drastically. To illustrate this point, let's say that during the ice ages, mammoths and other large herbivores feasted on a diet of plants A, B, and C. When the climate changed in the Late Pleistocene, plant A shifted northward to land where it could grow better. Meanwhile, plant B shifted westward, and plant C shifted southward. The ABC combination of plants was no longer available.

As plants became isolated and restricted to certain areas, so did herbivore populations. This could have had tragic consequences for mammoths and other large mammals. Segregated populations reduce crossbreeding between different populations and increase inbreeding. As a result, defective genes could have spread quickly through the animal populations, leading to eventual extinction. Even without inbreeding, the squeezing of mammoth habitat into smaller areas could have pushed the animals to extinction.

It is also possible that the ABC combination of plants provided a necessary mix of nutrients that the mammoths needed to survive. If mammoths moved to a place rich in plant A, they would not get the nutrients that only plants B and C contained. The result would have been dietary stress, which could have led to the animals' demise.

The climate model for extinction works especially well for the woolly mammoths in Eurasia. In Siberia, for example, the woolly mammoth was adapted to the arctic steppes—cold, dry grasslands. As temperatures warmed at the end of the Pleistocene, permafrost started melting. The arctic steppes gave way to mossy bogs with only small "islands" of grassland. As the climate became warmer and wetter, forests advanced, further reducing the woolly mammoth's grassland habitat.

Eventually, the steppes were replaced by boggy tundra in the north and coniferous forests in the south. The tundra's slow-growing, water-soaked clumps of mosses, sedges, and shrubs contained few nutrients. While reindeer and musk oxen could live on the tundra vegetation, woolly mammoths may have had a hard time surviving on such a diet.

The climate model doesn't hold up as well in other parts of the world. For example, in North America, the warmer, wetter climate encouraged grasslands to expand. Although these expanding grasslands may not have had the same mix of grasses that existed earlier, Columbian mammoths shouldn't have suffered much. They could easily migrate 100 miles (160 kilometers) or

Some scientists propose that a lack of diversity in grasslands may have contributed to the Columbian mammoth's mass extinction.

more in a matter of days. The animals could have spent time grazing on one kind of grass and then traveled to the next valley or hillside to munch on other vegetation.

Long migrations would have been more difficult for smaller mammals, so they would be expected to die off first. Although the summers were probably hotter and drier in North America, rivers like the present-day Missouri and Mississippi and their tributaries would have provided the animals—especially the ones that could easily travel long distances—with plenty of water.

There's another problem with the climate model of extinction. The Late Pleistocene interglacial was not the first warming period endured by mammoths and other now-extinct animals. Warming periods had occurred many times during the previous 1.7 million years. The Pleistocene was marked by at least twenty-two major climatic cycles and thousands of smaller ones, but there is no evidence of any other mass extinctions during that epoch.

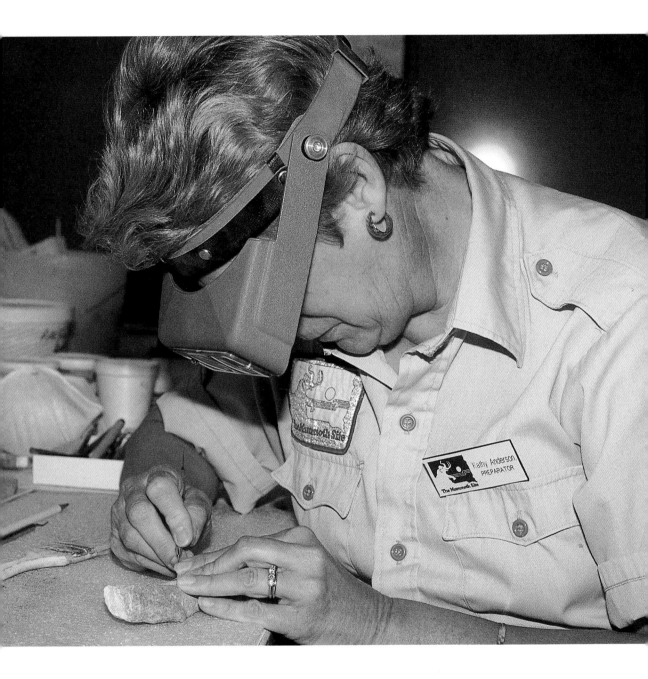

Chapter Eight

THE SEARCH FOR
ANSWERS CONTINUES

The overkill and overchill theories are the most accepted explanations of prehistoric extinction, but scientists have also developed some less conventional ideas. One such notion is that a mysterious killer virus or bacterium, spread by humans, made the mammoths ill and eventually killed them. This epidemic disease idea is sometimes called the overill theory. Did early humans, or the domesticated animals they brought with them as they migrated across the continents, carry germs that wiped out massive numbers of large animals? Perhaps.

When Christopher Columbus and other Europeans came to the Americas, they introduced a variety of diseases, including smallpox, to native peoples. Because the natives had never encountered the bacteria and viruses before, they had no immunity to them and thousands of people died.

Humans infecting other humans is one thing, but how likely is it that humans could infect other animals with a deadly virus? HIV (the virus that causes AIDS) and the deadly Ebola virus have demonstrated that a virus can indeed move from one species (monkeys) to another (humans). Thus, the overill theory suggests that when humans first came to North America, they or their domesticated animals, such as dogs, transmitted germs to large animals. Because the animals had never before

A laboratory technician at The Mammoth Site of Hot Springs prepares a mammoth bone for storage.

been exposed to human diseases, their bodies could not fight the germs. Large animals, such as mammoths, were most susceptible because they had so few young and took so long to reproduce.

The major problem with the overill theory is that no one has ever discovered a potential culprit. There is also no evidence that a virus or bacterium has ever wiped out an entire species.

DEATH BY COMET?

Many scientists believe that an extraterrestrial impact drove the dinosaurs to extinction sixty-five million years ago. So perhaps a comet or asteroid caused the Late Pleistocene mass extinction. There is quite a bit of evidence that a large space rock struck Earth shortly before the dinosaurs disappeared. Fine dust particles from the huge explosion were thrown into the air and became trapped there, preventing sunlight from reaching Earth's surface. The planet cooled, plants died, and so did the animals that ate the plants and the carnivores that ate the plant eaters. The result—extinction.

However, there is no concrete evidence that a similar event killed the mammoths. Additionally, if a comet or asteroid had crashed into Earth, extinction would have been quick and total. This is not what happened in the Late Pleistocene. Extinctions occurred over several thousand years, with a much greater loss of large animals in the Americas than in Eurasia.

NEW EVIDENCE

Scientists seem to be left with two equally plausible theories. Either human hunters or climatic change wiped out the mammoths, or perhaps it was a combination of both. Maybe the climatic and vegetation changes of the Late Pleistocene forced mammoths into increasingly smaller habitats, and in periods of drought, the isolated mammoth populations gathered around the few remaining watering holes. This would have made for relatively easy pickings by human hunters.

Because there is no clear answer, researchers continue to look for clues. Recently, new evidence from a study of mammoth tusks helped bolster the overkill theory.

A mammoth's tusks grew continuously throughout the animal's life. The calcium-rich dentin that made up the tusks formed a series of cones. As the cones stacked on top of one another, the tusks grew longer and longer. If you slice a mammoth tusk in half lengthwise, you can see layer upon layer of dentin. When plenty of food was available and the mammoth grew quickly, the dentin layers of its tusks were thick. During periods when the mammoth grew more slowly, the dentin layers were thinner.

By looking at the thickness and number of layers of dentin in a mammoth's tusks, researchers can draw conclusions about the animal's diet and reproductive activity, as well as about

A lengthwise cross section of a mammoth tusk clearly shows its stacked-cone structure.

the climate at the time. Tusk studies have shown that the growth rate of male mammoths dropped around the time they reached age ten. This reduced growth rate corresponds to the time when most males were kicked out of their family group. After several years, the youngsters learned to fend for themselves, and their growth rate recovered.

Growth patterns were different in young female mammoths. The females experienced no major decrease around age ten. Instead, they began demonstrating a regular rise and fall in tusk growth rate that apparently lasted throughout their reproductive life. This up-and-down tusk growth may have corre-

Tusks hold clues to the lives of mammoths.

sponded with the female's birthing cycle. In other words, tusk growth may have decreased during pregnancy and increased after giving birth.

Once researchers had a basic understanding of mammoth tusk patterns, they proposed that if mammoths were experiencing nutritional stress due to climate change, the dentin layers in their tusks should indicate that the animals were maturing later than normal and giving birth less often. These behavioral adaptations would be the mammoths' way of coping in an environment with limited food resources.

On the other hand, if mammoths were being stressed by human hunters, their tusks should show that the animals were maturing earlier and giving birth more often. This behavior would indicate that the mammoths were trying to replenish their numbers as quickly as possible. So far, studies of Columbian mammoth tusks suggest that, during the Late Pleistocene, the animals had plenty to eat and that their biggest threat was human hunters.

Chapter Nine

EXTINCTION—THEN AND NOW

Why should we be concerned when certain species, such as mammoths, become extinct? After all, many animals and plants have become extinct since life first appeared on Earth.

One reason we need to understand extinction is that, like other creatures, we are part of an intricate ecosystem. When even one species dies, it can set in motion a chain reaction that could destroy many other creatures. If humans do not protect other creatures, the day may come when we, too, will face extinction.

The extinction of the mammoths and other Ice-Age animals is especially significant because it is the first major die-off that occurred after humans evolved. If humans were responsible for, or contributed to, the mass extinction of the Late Pleistocene, what we learn about that event can help us live in harmony with the creatures that share our world.

There are many more humans on the planet than there were eleven thousand years ago. As we clear land to construct new buildings and raise livestock, other creatures lose their homes. Technological advances have made our lives easier, but they have also polluted our environment. Many of the animals that have lived on Earth for millions of years are in danger of becoming extinct. That means humans may be in trouble too.

Pollution from factories ruins our air and water. If we want to avoid the fate of mammoths, we need to examine the way we treat our environment.

There is also another reason to learn as much as we can about the Late Pleistocene extinctions. Some scientists believe that the ice ages aren't really over and that the time we're living in is just another interglacial. The glaciers may one day advance again across the continents. Whatever we discover about the mammoths of the past may teach us how to live in a changing environment in the future.

While it's too late to save mammoths, we may still be able to help their cousins—the elephants. African and Asian elephants are in grave danger of vanishing from Earth. For thousands of years, hunters killed these animals for their meat, hides, and tusks. Then, in the late 1800s and early 1900s, the killing escalated tremendously. Experts estimate that fewer than one hundred thousand elephants are left in the world.

By studying elephants, scientists have begun to understand their importance within their ecosystems. These giant animals often push over trees and clear away underbrush. This expands grassland areas and creates new habitats for other animals. Some people view this tree-removal behavior as destructive, but it's only destructive because humans have crowded the elephants into such small habitats. If elephants still roamed freely, their impact on any one area would be much less.

When elephants eat plants, the seeds pass through the animals' digestive tracts. In the process, they are carried to new places where they may have less competition for nutrients. The journey through the elephant's body may also help the seeds germinate better.

In addition, elephant dung is very important to an insect called the dung beetle, which obtains nutrients from and lays its eggs in the droppings. Because an elephant digests only about 44 percent of the food it eats, elephant dung is an excellent

A dung beetle rolls a ball of elephant dung. This beetle depends on elephants for its survival.

source of food for other creatures, such as baboons. The carcasses of elephants provide a major food source for vultures, jackals, hyenas, and insects. Lions and crocodiles often prey on young, sick, or dead elephants.

As elephants graze through grasses, they stir up insects and frogs, which birds eat. Elephants also dig waterholes that other animals use, and they excavate caves in search of salt. The holes they create may become homes to such animals as bats, birds, monkeys, and hyraxes.

Obviously, elephants contribute a great deal to their ecosystem. In fact, some researchers call them a keystone species, which means they improve conditions for other creatures by providing new or better resources. As long as humans confine elephants to smaller and smaller habitats and illegally kill elephants for their valuable ivory tusks, Earth's largest land animals will continue to face extinction. If elephants disappear, what will happen to all the other living things that depend on them?

Like modern elephants, mammoths were one of the largest mammals to ever live on land—graceful giants among animals. They were also very intelligent creatures. Like elephants, mammoths almost certainly had an advanced communication system that involved touch, smell, and sound, as well as a social order as sophisticated as that of humans. They lived in family groups whose members took care of one another. When one animal died, the others mourned and even wept. Mammoth calves were protected and nurtured, and adults taught the youngsters how to survive.

Like elephants and modern humans, mammoths and Ice-Age people had much in common. Both had long lifespans, and their young had lengthy childhoods that gave them plenty of time to learn from experience. Pregnancies were long, and females stopped giving birth around age forty-five to fifty. Both fell victim to diseases of the heart and to arthritis.

Mammoths were vitally important to the Ice-Age people. Early humans depended on mammoths for shelter, food, clothing, tools, and weaponry. Pleistocene art and religious artifacts reveal a reverence for these Ice-Age titans. If it hadn't been for mammoths, people might not have arrived in the Americas until much later—perhaps not until the eighth century A.D., when the seafaring Vikings landed. Mammoths arrived here first, but Paleo-Indian hunters were hot on their trail.

Extinction is an inevitable process in nature. Creatures will always find ways to evolve features that give them an advantage over other living things. However, humans have the ability to influence, change, and disrupt this natural progression. What are the short-term and long-term consequences of this? It is important to carefully consider this question because extinction is permanent, and as the saying goes, you don't know what you have until it's gone. We've lost the great mammoths, but perhaps we can still save elephants and other species that help maintain the balance of nature.

CAN MAMMOTHS BE RESURRECTED?

Is extinction really the last chapter in the story of the mammoth? Perhaps not. In 1997 the remains of a frozen woolly mammoth were discovered in the Siberian permafrost. In 1999 the mammoth—still embedded in ice—was taken to a study site in Khatanga, Russia. The Discovery Channel filmed the excavation and, in March 2000, aired a globally televised documentary, *Raising the Mammoth*. The program detailed the first excavation of mammoth remains completely entombed in ice. Previous excavations of mammoths from the permafrost usually entailed melting the ice with hot-water hoses. Unfortunately, this method typically destroyed the soft tissues of the animal, leaving only the skeletal remains.

The Jarkov mammoth, named for the Siberian family of the Dolgan tribe that discovered it, was carved from the frozen earth and airlifted in its 23-ton (24-metric-ton) ice coffin. The mammoth is stored in a permafrost tunnel beneath the streets of Khatanga. Scientists have yet to discover how much of the mammoth's body is contained in the ice block.

Eventually, scientists hope to find out how the animal died; examine vegetation in its stomach and intestines; search the body for possible parasites, bacteria, viruses, or other microbes;

Scientists hope the Jarkov mammoth (shown here entombed in ice in a permafrost tunnel), discovered in 1997 in Siberia, will provide clues to Earth's history.

determine the size, shape, and volume of the internal organs; and study any insect and plant remains trapped in the permafrost surrounding the mammoth. In addition to these studies, some scientists want to try to recover and clone some of the mammoth's DNA to create a living twenty-first-century twin.

To clone the Jarkov mammoth, intact DNA from the mammoth could be injected into the nucleus of an Asian elephant cell to produce a modern-day woolly mammoth. This is the same method that was used to produce Dolly, a sheep cloned in Scotland in 1997. Scientists might also be able to use sperm from the mammoth to fertilize the egg of an elephant. If successful, the baby would be 50 percent elephant and 50 percent mammoth. It would take several generations of breeding before scientists could produce a woolly mammoth that looked like its ancient ancestor using this method. Both methods currently seem impossible.

Scientists do not know whether enough DNA or sperm are present in the specimen for cloning to work. In addition, there are ethical issues to consider. Should an extinct Ice-Age animal be brought back to life?

Scientists do not yet know whether the Jarkov mammoth will provide answers to all their questions. Even if it doesn't, researchers know there are many more mammoths—perhaps thousands—buried in the permafrost of Siberia. At least scientists have the methodology and techniques to recover and preserve these Ice-Age giants for future research.

A scientist examines DNA patterns. This process may be used in mammoth research.

GLOSSARY

archaeologist: a scientist who studies prehistoric and ancient human cultures

carnivore: an animal that hunts and kills other animals for food

clone: to produce a genetically identical copy of an organism

coniferous: cone-bearing, such as pine, spruce, or hemlock trees

crossbreed: to mate two varieties or breeds within the same species

deinothere: an extinct proboscidean with downward-curving lower tusks

dentin: hard, calcium-rich tissue under the enamel of a tooth

desiccation: drying out; dehydration

DNA: the abbreviation for deoxyribonucleic acid, the molecule that contains an organism's genetic material and controls the production of proteins

elephantid: a member of the family Elephantidae; a subgroup of proboscideans

evolve: to change slowly over time

extinction: death of the last surviving member of a species

fossil: remains, impressions, or traces of a living thing from a past geologic age

gomphothere: a primitive proboscidean that is not directly related to mammoths or mastodons

herbivore: an animal that eats only plants

hyoid bone: a support bone located at the base of a mammal's tongue

inbreed: to mate with closely related individuals

incisor: a front tooth; in proboscideans, the two upper incisors are called tusks

interglacial a period of warmer temperatures between glacial advances

mammutid: a member of the family Mastodontidae, a subgroup of proboscideans

matriarchal society: a social organization in which a female is the head of the family group

midden: a pile of material, such as the nest of a pack rat

molar: one of the grinding teeth in the upper and lower jaws of some animals

mollusk: an animal, such as a clam or snail, with a soft body and usually an outer shell

mummify: to dry and preserve a dead body

overchill theory: the hypothesis that climate change caused the extinction of mammoths

overill theory: the hypothesis that an epidemic disease caused the extinction of mammoths

overkill theory: the hypothesis that hunting by prehistoric humans caused the extinction of mammoths

Paleo-Indian: an early human who lived in the Americas more than six thousand years ago

paleontologist: a scientist who studies evidence of past life on Earth

parasite: an organism living on, with, or in another organism

permafrost: a permanently frozen underground layer of earth

petroglyph: a prehistoric pecking or carving on rock

Pleistocene epoch: the period of Earth's history that began 1.8 million years ago and ended 10,000 years ago. This epoch was marked by advancing and retreating glaciers and is also known as the Ice Age.

proboscidean: a large mammal with a long, flexible snout

radiocarbon dating: a method of determining the age of a fossil by measuring the ratio of naturally occurring carbon 12 atoms to radioactive carbon 14 atoms in the specimen

species: a group of organisms that have common characteristics and can mate and produce healthy young

steppe: an extensive, semiarid grassland without trees

vertebra (plural vertebrae): one of the bones that forms the backbone or spinal column of an animal

FOR FURTHER READING

BOOKS

Agenbroad, L. D. *Pygmy (Dwarf) Mammoths of the Channel Islands of California*. Hot Springs, SD: The Mammoth Site of Hot Springs, South Dakota, Inc., 1998.

Augusta, J. *A Book of Mammoths*. London: Paul Hamlyn Ltd., 1963.

Cohen, Daniel. *Cloning*. New York: Twenty-First Century, 1998.

Klein, R. G. *Ice Age Hunters of the Ukraine*. Chicago: University of Chicago Press, 1973.

Lister, A., and P. Bahn. *Mammoths*. New York: Macmillan, 1994.

Mol, D., L. Agenbroad, and J. Mead. *Mammoths*. Hot Springs, SD: The Mammoth Site of Hot Springs, South Dakota, Inc., 1993.

Nelson, L. W. *Mammoth Graveyard: A Treasure Trove of Clues of the Past*. Hot Springs, SD: The Mammoth Site of Hot Springs, South Dakota, Inc., 1988.

Silverberg, R. *Mammoths, Mastodons, and Man*. Kingswood, England: World's Work Ltd., 1970.

Smith, Norman. *Millions and Billions of Years Ago: Dating Our Earth and Its Life*. Danbury, CT: Franklin Watts, 1993.

Sutcliffe, A. J. *On the Track of Ice Age Mammals*. London: British Museum of Natural History, 1985.

Thompson, Sharon Elaine. *Death Trap: The Story of the La Brea Tar Pits*. Minneapolis, MN: Lerner, 1994.

Vergoth, Karin, and Christopher Lampton. *Endangered Species*. Danbury, CT: Franklin Watts, 1999.

ONLINE SITES

Mammoths
<http://www.museum.state.il.us/exhibits/larson/mammuthus.html>
Check out this site created and maintained by the Illinois State Museum to learn a variety of basic facts about mammoths that inhabited North America.

Mammoth Saga (Swedish Natural History Museum)
<http://www.nrm.se/virtexhi/mammsaga/>
This site offers a virtual tour of the Swedish Museum of Natural History's exhibit of mammoths and other Ice-Age plants and animals. Be sure to check out links to information on mammoths, including how they adapted to cold weather and theories of their extinction.

Mammoth Site of Hot Springs
<http://www.mammothsite.com/>
This is the official home page of the South Dakota excavation site described in Chapter Four. You can take a cybertour of the museum and view photos of the excavation site. There is even a link to a puzzle page.

The Page Museum at the La Brea Tar Pits
<http://www.tarpits.org/>
This is the official home page of the La Brea Tar Pits in Los Angeles, described in Chapter Four. Check out this site to get a virtual tour of the park, see the variety of Ice-Age animals whose fossils have been found in the tar pits, and view the Gilbert family collection of photographs documenting the early excavation of the site.

Raising the Mammoth
<http://www.discovery.com/exp/mammoth/mammoth.html>
This site features a variety of information about the 1999 Siberian mammoth excavation mentioned in Chapter Nine of this book.

Woolly Mammoth
<http://school.discovery.com/schooladventures/woollymammoth/>
Visit this site to learn fun facts about woolly mammoths. This site includes a migration map, a timeline, web links, and a quiz to test your knowledge of woolly mammoths.

INDEX

PHOTO ACKNOWLEDGMENTS

The photographs and illustrations in this book are reproduced courtesy of, Dr. Larry D. Agen-broad, pp. 1, 2–3, 13, 26, 57, 60, 62 (right), 63 (both), 64, 68, 80, 93 (both); The Mammoth Site of Hot Springs, South Dakota, pp. 2, 30; Kathy Anderson, The Mammoth Site of Hot Springs, South Dakota, pp. 10, 32 (left), 79, 104; John C. Dawson, courtesy of the George C. Page Museum, pp. 6, 15 (left); AP World Wide Photos, pp. 8, 32 (right), 53, 58, 77; illustrations by Laura Westlund, pp. 14, 23; Paula Jansen, pp. 15 (right), 17, 19, 27, 28, 36 (both), 46, 49 (both), 52, 62 (left), 70, 78, 92 (both), 99, 100; © Mark Hallett, pp. 16, 35, 51, 88; © Charles & Josette Lenars/CORBIS, p. 20; © Olivier Blaise/Gamma Press Inc., p. 24; © Arthur Morris/Visuals Un-limited, p. 25; © Reuters NewMedia Inc./CORBIS, p. 33; D. C. Fisher, University of Michigan, pp. 34, 103; The Natural History Museum, London, pp. 37, 83, 84, 91; © Joe McDonald/COR-BIS, p. 38; © Gallo Images/CORBIS, pp. 39, 109; Courtesy of the George C. Page Museum, pp. 40, 54, 56; © Mark Newman/Visuals Unlimited, p. 41; © Jonathan Blair/CORBIS, p. 43; © Richard T. Nowitz/CORBIS, p. 44; Mary Butler, courtesy of the George C. Page Museum, p. 55; The Art Archive/Dagli Orti, p. 70 (inset); © Bettmann/CORBIS, p. 71; © Staffan Wid-strand/CORBIS, p. 72; © R. Sheridan, Ancient Art and Architecture Collection, Ltd., p. 74; Michael Long, The Natural History Museum, London, p. 86; © Premium Stock/CORBIS, p. 106; © AFP/CORBIS, p. 112; © Simon Fraser/Science Photo Library/Photo Researchers, Inc., p. 113. Cover photo is used courtesy of the Mammoth Site of Hot Springs, South Dakota.

ABOUT THE AUTHORS

Dr. Larry Agenbroad holds a bachelor's degree in geological engineering and advanced degrees in geology and anthropology. He is a professor of geology at Northern Arizona University and splits his time between homes in Flagstaff, Arizona, and Hot Springs, South Dakota. His wife and two sons often help him with his fieldwork and research.

Dr. Agenbroad's mammoth adventures began more than thirty-five years ago, when he helped excavate two sites in southeastern Arizona. In the 1970s, Dr. Agenbroad discovered an area now known as The Mammoth Site of Hot Springs, South Dakota. Scientists found tons of mammoth bones resting in the earth, lying in the same spots where the animals had died or where their bones were deposited thousands of years earlier.

In 1983 Dr. Agenbroad and his colleague Jim Mead discovered the first complete specimens of mammoth dung in the Western Hemisphere. For the first time, they could compare the diet of mammoths that had lived in the southwestern United States to that of frozen mammoths from Siberia.

Dr. Agenbroad subsequently led the excavation of the world's most complete pygmy mammoth skeleton on Santa Rosa Island, off the coast of California. Most recently he traveled to Siberia to help recover a woolly mammoth entombed in ice. Some scientists hope this animal might yield the DNA necessary to clone a woolly mammoth. The excavation and recovery of the mammoth were featured in a documentary produced for and aired on the Discovery Channel in 2000.

Lisa Nelson received a bachelor's degree in journalism from Northern Arizona University. She caught the mammoth bug when she was assigned to write articles about Dr. Agenbroad's research for Northern Arizona University's News and Publications Office. She lives in Flagstaff, Arizona, with her husband and their two horses.

She says, "Dinosaurs have long captured the imagination of children and adults alike. But when you stroke an elegantly curved ivory tusk or run your fingers along the ridges of teeth that munched on grass twenty-six thousand years ago, you're immediately transported back to a time when mammoths and humans shared a destiny. Suddenly, you are overcome by a sense of loss for what is no longer." Ms. Nelson currently is director of Creative Communications at Northern Arizona University.